The Crowded Table

THE BRAVE AND BEAUTIFUL CHOICE TO MOTHER MANY

52 Women Share Their Stories

ANGELA CONNELLY

Inspira
LITERARY SOLUTIONS

The Crowded Table: The Brave and Beautiful Choice to Mother Many
First Edition Trade Book, 2022
© 2022 Angela Connelly

To order additional books:
www.angelaconnelly.com
www.amazon.com

ISBN: 978-1-952943-15-7

Editorial and Book Production: Inspira Literary Solutions, Gig Harbor, Washington
Book Design: Brianna Showalter, Ruston, Washington

Throughout this book you will see a mix of personal, professional, and stock photos—too many to try to credit and caption individually. Thank you to the contributors who submitted many wonderful photos with their writings. Quite a few of those photos are included here; others could not be used. We have done our best to try to represent them well where personal photos could not be used.

Printed in the USA by Ingram Spark.

My friends, ABUNDANCE awaits us all.

"Abundance" is what the crowded table represents.

This prayer and this book are for EVERYONE.

We are called to be fruitful.

Each of us is uniquely summoned to be the broken-open seed that gives life…

spiritually, emotionally, biologically.

Let us all daringly embrace a life of "fiat," of saying yes

to birthing many in all the ways God whispers to us.

And again, like Teresa, a prolific spiritual mother, states,

"May you trust God that you are exactly where you are meant to be."

May today there be peace within.

May you trust God that you are exactly where you are meant to be.

May you not forget the infinite possibilities that are born of faith.

May you use those gifts that you have received and pass on the love
that has been given to you.

May you be content knowing that you are a child of God.

Let this presence settle into your bones and allow your soul the freedom
to sing, dance, praise, and love.

It is there for each and every one of us.

– Saint Teresa of Avila

"May God give us all openness to ways leading
beyond our own selves."

— Mother Teresa

The Crowded Table is dedicated
to every woman throughout time who has:

- ~ rocked the cradle
- ~ done the dishes
- ~ made the beds
- ~ set the table
- ~ kissed the scrapes and bruises
- ~ wiped the tears
- ~ embraced the broken
- ~ fed the multitudes
- ~ washed the feet
- ~ held the dying
- ~ allowed her body and spirit to be a conduit of life and love and hope for her home and for the world.

Table of Contents

Welcome!—to a wild cultural ride of women, lifestyle choices, love, babies, declining birth rates, and big bounteous families...

PART 5 – BURSTING AT THE SEAMS WITH LOVE   135

PART 6 – THE NEVER-ENDING FRUITFUL GARDEN   159

PART 7 – SCIENCE SPEAKS   179

Acknowledgments

I want to first thank every woman who gives life—spiritually, physically, and in every way her day may bring. Let us all continue to give life, setting the crowded table where all are welcome and all are loved, and continue speaking life and birthing love until our final breath. You are the true inspiration for this book!

I want to thank the village that has made the tiny bud of a book sprouting in my soul to flower so fruitfully. This village includes first the 52 heroic women in these pages, some of the busiest humans in the world, who sat down and shared their tears and joys of their uncommon large family life. They have shared their vulnerability and their gifts. And, amongst the dishes and laundry they found a way... these woman can do anything!!!

I want to thank my husband, Jack, and my nine kids, my very own village, who have weathered many an adventure of their passionate mom's escapades in community advocacy. I apologize for all the times I have not literally set that table, and you've fended for yourselves. I believe, though, it's part of why you all are so resilient! You know how to buck up! And, as you all surmise, your mama's escapades are not ending. This book adventure is just the latest!!! And it won't be the last, ☺. Thank you ahead of time!

I also want to thank, as well, all the families of each of these heroic women. You husbands and children in all of our large families—although you all are accustomed to our multitasking—you probably never imagined that this was what was happening after you were all in bed, or when Mom was distracted on her phone waiting in the carpool line.

I particularly want to thank the rockstar dream team that made this anthology happen in a brick-and-mortar way!!! Aubrianna, my wonderful technical assistant—thank you; you know technology is one of my greatest weaknesses!!! And Arlyn Lawrence and Heather Sipes at Inspira Literary Solutions; thank you for patiently embracing my crazy-busy life and my inattention to detail…and walking me through each step of the publishing process with deep and kind patience. And, for prodding me on when I needed it!

Ultimately I want to thank the Birther of all Life and Love, God Himself! You have helped us all be cocreators in Your magnificent plan of humanity! Jesus, You came that we may have life, and have it abundantly (John 10:10). Thank you, God, for Beauty and Goodness and Joy.

And thank you, Mother Mary…for showing us the way with your *fiat* ("yes") to Life.

Our world cries out for our motherhood, friends. May we all mother on beyond every border.

Introduction

I write this book as a happy and humbled mom of a big, rowdy family.

I write from the chaos of the kitchen, amongst the messy counters and the loud, wrestling boys on the rug.

I write this book from a laughable lack of technological skill, and a much-too-long to-do list.

And that is why it's the right time to write this book.

I will never be enough, my family will never behave perfectly enough, the house will never be clean enough, and the clock will never tick slowly enough.

But it's in moments exactly like these when God shows up.

It's in those realizations of our smallness and insufficiency that love and grace find a way in.

It's actually completely freeing: God is taking care of it all.

When we surrender ourselves—when we unclench our fists and open our hearts—that's when the steam of grace flows freely, and that's why saying "yes" to mothering (and saying it over and over again) is so sweet.

Mothering many is beyond
the norm,
mothering many is beyond
our two hands,
and therein lies the magic,
and therein lies the joy,
and therein lies the beauty!

I have nine rambunctious kids—seven boys in a row between my two strong girls.

"Authentic Beauty unlocks the yearning of the human heart, the profound desire to know, to love, to go toward the Other, to reach for the Beyond."

— Pope Benedict XVI

Yes, I know where babies come from. Yes, they are all mine, and yes, I always wanted a big family. Yes, my hands are full, and my heart is even fuller. Finally, yes, even though my choice is uncommon and unconventional in today's world of declining birth rates, I enjoy a true sense of liberation, deep gratitude, and overflowing abundance. I have made the choice to say "yes" to mothering many in an age of fewer babies.

There are many like me who experience the wonderful joy of a large family. This book is about women who have made this choice and the importance of their choice. This book intends to take you on a wild ride about women, life, love, varying views of feminism, family, history and statistics relating to birth rates, and the intentional choice to mother many children in the midst of it all.

When birth rates decline, populations reach a point at which they fail to replace themselves, and as women have fewer babies—and have them later in life—these are critically important conversations for the global community.

This choice by some to mother many should be fully honored and supported. We are living in a time when the ability to listen is becoming increasingly important. Now is the time to listen and learn from each other, and to give all women a voice and a seat at the table, including women who choose to mother many.

MEET SOME AMAZING MOTHERS

My intent within these pages is to introduce you to an amazing and wide-ranging circle of women from around the world who have deliberately made this choice. These 52 women speak out, transparently sharing their hearts, their personal choices, and the challenges and joys of raising big families. They are honest, diverse, and very real moms. They have chosen to birth, to nurture, and to raise large families. These women, most of whom have four or more kids, are strong, interesting, educated, world-impacting women from Washington State to Washington D.C., from Guatemala to Nigeria.

Though each woman and her story is unique, they all share the belief that a life filled with many young children brims with beauty and joy, even in the chaos, and that this decision is totally, fundamentally, and profoundly worthwhile.

The 52 women within these pages stand out as loving mothers as well as doctors, professors, vintners, social workers, editors, authors, homeschooling moms, and more. They each uniquely share their choice to say "yes" to mothering many in a world of fewer babies.

In *The Crowded Table*, the raw, authentic glimpses of life represent a lifestyle choice that is often unfamiliar, and sometimes misunderstood and marginalized, on the world stage. We live in an era that has decreased the value of motherhood and diminished the stature of women everywhere around the world who say "yes" to mothering large families. Their voices are needed on the world stage.

This current "societal disapproval" of larger-than-average families has led to a decreasing population. Scientists from around the world are sounding the alarm: many cultures are no longer achieving replacement rates. According to the CDC, the average birth rate in the United States is 1.73 children per family (2018), below the replacement rate necessary for a generation to replace itself, and for society's continuation.[1]

1 https://www.cdc.gov/mmwr/volumes/69/wr/mm6901a5.htm

Women are having fewer babies. Countries must rely on fewer citizens and are consequently having trouble finding people to care for their aging populations.

In his book *What to Expect When No One's Expecting*, author Jonathan V. Last writes about "America's Coming Demographic Disaster."[2]

Last notes:

- Birth rates have declined around the world.
- In Japan, people buy more adult diapers than they do diapers for babies.
- In Italy, there are already more deaths than births each year.
- China's one-child policy has left the country with an impending population contraction that has the ruling class terrified.
- The Center for Disease Control (CDC) has just declared that birth rates in the U.S. are at their lowest point in 42 years.[3]

Scientifically and demographically, there's a worldwide baby bust! If America wants to continue to lead the world in its brain trust, its workforce, and its cultural, economic, and social richness, we need to have more babies.

We are currently living in an era that often devalues motherhood and discourages women from saying "yes" to mothering many. It's time for a cultural "opening of the mind" and honest dialogue. Instead of criticism and intolerance, it's time to be inclusive and open to hearing about these women and their choices—in

2 Last, Jonathan V. *What to Expect When No One's Expecting: America's Coming Demographic Disaster.* New York, NY: Encounter Books, 2014.

3 Vital Statistics Rapid Release. (n.d.). Retrieved February 6, 2022, from https://www.cdc.gov/nchs/data/vsrr/vsrr012-508.pdf

> *"The circles of women around us weave invisible nets of love that carry us when we are weak and sing with us when we are strong."*
>
> *— Sark*

their own voices—and to give them a seat at the global table and learn about their worthwhile adventures in a world suffering from too few babies.

TIMING IS CRITICAL

The conversation has started. Not long ago, at a Gates Foundation conference, French President Emmanuel Macron voiced an often-heard belief about the "type" of women who have large families. Macron, somewhat condescendingly, noted, "As I always say, show me a fully educated lady who would choose to have seven, eight, or nine children."

In response, Dr. Catherine Pakaluk, economics professor from Harvard and Catholic University of America, who made the choice to mother eight children, sent President Macron a postcard with a picture of her and her many children. This started the Twitter-viral phenomenon called *#post-cardsformacron*. An avalanche of women who had chosen to mother many sent in postcards with photos showing their big, beautiful families.

The Crowded Table and the stories of these women it contains are intended to continue the critical conversation and to respond to those who, like Macron, question the choice to mother many. The voices of these strong mothers represent a vitally important part of the ongoing global conversation on mothering, the world's crisis of too few babies, and the need to listen to differing viewpoints in this arena.

In *The Crowded Table*, 52 mothers of large families offer a hope-filled, unique, welcoming, faithful, honest, and desperately needed new perspective on the cul-

Seeing a hidden beauty in the mess,
Hearing a sweet song
in the clutter of the noise,
Finding a deep peace in the storm
Of everyday life.

tural norms concerning women, life, love, and children. Significantly, these are real and imperfect women with real and imperfect families, and though often holding many balls in the air at once, we love this daring life of abundance.

Whether or not mothering many would be your choice, I assure you, this cultural ride is worthwhile, interesting, and entertaining. And know that no matter what, you are with friends.

THE GIFT OF SISTERHOOD

One of the gifts of this connection with these trailblazing women is the commitment to walking with all our sisters through the good and the bad times. When you mother many, your heart breaks open, and you realize that every child is your child, and every mother out there is your sister!

This is why a percentage of the proceeds from *The Crowded Table* will go to nonprofit organizations that are helping moms and babies who are in the trenches. It's a circle of friends from all over the world—we are here, and we are united in our purpose to help families thrive. As moms of many, we are in on a secret. Love is not quantitative; it grows and expands the more you give it! There's always room for more love. It's amazing what sisters can do when they roll up their sleeves together!

by Justin Connelly

The Hard and the Holy

*We rejoice in our sufferings, knowing that suffering produces endur-
ance, and endurance produces character, and character produces hope.
Romans 5:3-4*

We all have a story to tell: stories of pain, heartbreak, and deep woundedness. We also all have journeys of resurrections and great joy! A wise mama of many once said, "Everyone is five seconds from tears if you truly know them."

In our call to mothering, we are the warm blanket and the shoulder to cry on; we hold their hair back when our loved ones are sick; we clean up the blood, the sweat, and the tears. At the end of the day, we carry our loved ones home. Though on the surface everyone is "fine," our mama eyes and hearts see deeper into the heavy, hidden load that each one carries.

As women, as mothers—biologically, spiritually, emotionally—our hearts and souls have been empowered to enter into the woundedness, to embrace and hold the pain of those we love, and of the hurting of the world. And by doing so, we can be instruments of healing. Uniquely, we mothers are called to be the hands and feet of Christ, bravely treading into the pain. In the darkest moments, we are called to be Mary, as in Michelangelo's *Pieta*, holding her murdered son.

You are about to meet 11 women in Part 1 of this book who have faced the hard and the holy and have been called to hold it all. They have faced every imaginable heartache and challenge and, though broken time and again, they've made it through.

My own story includes journeys of the hard and the holy. The first of the stories you will read in this section is the story of my own "breaking open." As I held my dying, 27-year-old husband in my arms, with our two young babies nestled next to us, I never anticipated I'd be writing this book on mothering many.

Now, years later, a mother of nine, it is the knowledge that I was being tenderly held, in the hardest moments of my life, that I now proclaim loudly: God is good, and He wraps us in love and comfort, especially in our darkest hours. He holds us up with His own hands when we cannot stand on our own.

And that is why "The Hard and the Holy—Holding It All" is the first part of this book, because we begin from a place of knowing that *no matter what*, no matter how hard and impossible a situation is, no matter how weak and incompetent we feel, God will be there, in the center of the hurt.

And yes, there are some days, in those dark moments, when all we can do is crawl out of bed and show up. All these women crawled out of bed and showed up, in the hardest and holiest times of their lives… they held it all, and surrendered it to God and God held it all.

Mother love.

Angela Connelly

Angela is the mother of nine children, and an active community service advocate and communicator. She lives in Tacoma, Washington.

One of my boys was still asleep when the photographer of this picture arrived at our home for the photo shoot. Another one didn't get the memo to wear a black shirt, and…you see the guy with the huge smile in the back row? It's fake. And he has smiled that exact fake grin in every family photo we have ever taken.

This is us.

I honestly must say, though, when I look into the eyes of each of my children, I feel incredibly vulnerable. A mother suffers what each child suffers, is challenged by each of their struggles, and is elated by each of their joys. It's as if a mama's heart is splintered into the many shards of humanity that are her children.

But it is in this very breaking open, this very vulnerability, that we birth TRUE LOVE. And TRUE JOY. I want to declare loudly that love is so much more than candy and roses.

She broke the bread into two fragments
and gave them to the children, who ate with avidity.
"She hath kept none for herself," grumbled the Sergeant.
"Because she is not hungry," said a soldier.
"Because she is a mother," said the Sergeant.
– VICTOR HUGO

The Connelly Clan

It's also the thorns, the hard stuff, the messy and painful times, as well as all the beauty, fun, and joy!

And my mama's heart is so THANK-FUL for it all. It is so dang worth it! Let us be unafraid to love fiercely!

THE HARD AND HOLY ROAD

We are all on a journey.

We are fellow travelers, sojourning to-gether in this one wild and precious life.

We are linked with our spouses, our chil-dren, our parents, our communities, and all those lying, helpless, in our paths.

The question arises,

"Where are we all going?"

We are all walking each other home.

I learned this lesson acutely as a young wife and mother. My strong, faith-brim-ming, 26-year-old husband, Jon Syren, a third-year medical school student at the University of Washington, was suddenly diagnosed with cancer. And life suddenly slammed to a stop.

We were paralyzed, numb; we kept inch-ing forward, barely. This was not in any way what we were expecting. You see, we were going to do God's will. We felt called to give ourselves to great things; we had two little babies and we so wanted to help the world, heal the broken, create community, and have a gaggle of children.

Well, God whispered in the night, "There's more to the plan," and let us know that the goal of life is to walk each other home.

Through Jon's illness and death, that strong young man, stripped piece by piece of his dreams and goals, of all in this world, surrendered it all with iron love and faith, and beautifully walked home! He died peacefully, the youngest of the eight Syren siblings, in his Alaskan family home, surrounded by the loving hearts and helping hands of everyone in that big family. God was showing me what life was really about through Jon's journey home.

And, in the midst of it, I experienced to my core the gift of a big family. I was numb, standing alone, not knowing which way to turn. As a single mom I started to proceed, step by step, still in shock—and then stopped in my tracks. I had no idea what was next. All I could do was trust like a two-year-old and cling to my Father's hand. He took care of me, helped me and my babies heal, and so did my "doctor" in Heaven, Jon.

A couple of miles further down life's winding road, I was teaching a class at St Patrick's church in Tacoma, Washington, when a strong, faith-brimming young man came to my class. His name was John,

also, but everyone called him Jack.

Jack Connelly was a justice-hearted lawyer who felt a call to do great things. He wanted to heal the world and create community and loved the idea of a gaggle of children. We married, Jack adopted my two little ones, and we've had seven more—our abundant Connelly clan.

God brought beauty out of the ashes.

We try, every day, to do our best to help the world, to heal the world, to create justice and community for all. Every day has different challenges. We hope and pray our nine kids love those things too (we fail miserably all the time, and our kids are all on their own journeys, but thankfully, God writes straight with crooked lines).

And the perspective we have, especially from our wounds and living the hard stuff of life, is to try and never forget that the real meaning of this winding, wild journey, is *walking each other home…*

Karen Irwin

Karen is a journalist and editor, and the mother of four children.

The day I found out Kate's prognosis, I crawled under the covers in the middle of the afternoon and said, "Lord, I cannot do this. I cannot watch my child die. Please, please take me now."

Almost immediately a voice said, and I swear it was almost audible, "You get out of bed right now. You are a mother, not just on good days but on all days. Get downstairs and do what needs to be done."

That message sobered me up. I jumped out of bed and for the next two years I showed up in whatever capacity Kate and her siblings needed. I won't lie. Mother's Day is hard and it probably always will be. To be there for a child's both first and last breath is an experience I would wish on no one, but in the end, Kate and I shared a secret smile, because we knew not even death could break such a powerful and sacred connection.

Love wins. It really does.

I feel so very blessed to be called "Mom" by my amazing kids—I love them so, so much—and I'm so thankful to every person, every woman and man, who gets out of bed and shows up for each other, who does what needs to be done. That's mama love. We celebrate you today.

Christy Wall

Christy is the mother of nine children. She is a photographer, a rancher, a storyteller, and was once a paralegal.

While my children were growing up, I had a vague idea of how I was going to raise them and what was important.

I would teach them that character mattered. They needed to be honest, hardworking, and kind. I would teach them that family was important.

I would raise my children with faith—not a faith of rules and regulations, but a faith of love and devotion. When our oldest son, Franz, was recently paralyzed in a catastrophic ski accident, a dear friend of mine said, "He will be fine, and you will see that he has qualities you raised him with." There was that moment, hour, month of panic, where as a mother I thought, *And what was that? What did I raise him with?*

Now I see.

I see him cling to his faith, like a drowning man clings to a life raft in a great storm. I see him grasp again and again at the knowledge that God loves him, even if he can't see it. I see him cling to his knowledge of God and consider how best to serve Him. And most of all, I see him blindly, with arms reaching out, love God.

I see him look at his body, as we did with our great games, and figure out what he has to work with. I see him fixing problems so he can do the best with what he has.

But the best thing I see is his brothers and sisters circling around him, and doing what they can to protect him.

When he was depressed, I sent him his brother, Matthew, the great melancholic, to listen to him and cry with him, to give Franz a chance to let his grief out and to absorb it, like cutting open a poisonous wound and letting it drain.

I sent Analise, so full of kindness and sympathy, to wash the wound with utmost care. I sent Katie, the lovely, soothing Katie, who is like the sweetest balm on any wound.

Then I sent Margaret and Bernadette—the cheerful cholerics, who happily stitched it up, while laughing and joking. Then Bernhard, who put on the final bandage, the gleaming white cloth, making it look clean and smart again.

And finally, the two boys, to draw funny faces on the bandage to make Franz laugh and remember how to play.

And now, as I watch Franz, who, with sparkling eyes, struggles and fights for independence, I see what my friend said I would see. I see how it is that I raised my children. And, I am thankful.

It is by God's sweetness that He helped me raise my children, and by my husband's wisdom. It is by those little moments when we had to make a decision this way or that, that I made the choice that gave my children the tools to live.

Franz got a fresh haircut today. When he looked in the mirror, he said, his eyes glistening with emotion, "I'm back! Out of the wilderness!"

This has been a great week for Franz! When he had his first bite of food, he sighed, "Now life is worth living!" We are always corporeal beings first! He had Chicken Marsala from Italy, quiche from

France, a drenched burrito from Mexico, and Taco Bell from America! Intercontinental dining at its best.

Best of all, Franz is himself, joking, telling stories, trying to game the system and invent faster ways of doing things. He is talking with and encouraging the other folk who walk the same journey as he does. (The nurses already asked him to stay and work there.)

He's also been asked to join the Veteran's Paralytic Games. They see the heart of my boy, the heart of a lion.

Franz even gave advice to his baby sister in college: "Take this time to really strengthen your faith. Go to daily Mass, frequent confession. Learn your faith and make it yours. Life will throw you surprises, and your faith will need to be strong to handle it. Take it from me; college is the best time to really embrace your faith." There was a very humble assent on the other end of the phone.

And so this mom and dad sit, at their 29th anniversary, well pleased and thankful to God, as well as for the prayers of so many, which have given us strength!

Manola Secaira

Manola is a dentist and homemaker. Born and raised in Guatemala, she now lives in Washington State with her husband and eight children.

Since I can remember, my mom has been my hero. She has always been strong, witty, beautiful, and wickedly cool. She went to college; I wanted to go to college. She and my dad had four kids; I wanted to have four kids.

My first year of college, I heard someone say they wanted to have lots of kids. I saw the eyes of most of the listeners popping out of their heads, so I quickly said that I wanted four or six kids myself. But, just as Haydn, the Austrian composer, composed Symphony No. 94 just to see the ladies in the audience jump from their seats, so I later bumped my number to eight, just to see the faces of horror when I would proclaim this desire. It made me laugh. As time went by, I decided that it was actually a great idea to have many kids—in fact, as many as God would want me to have. And I was lucky enough to fall in love with a brilliant-

ly funny guy who was willing to embark on crazy adventures—like this one.

After graduation, we got married, moved to a different country, and started our family. By the time our fifth child was born, we had five kids under the age of five. Crazy times. (We also had two miscarriages, so then we had help from our little ones in Heaven.) Then came Paulina.

Paulina was born with a balanced translocation of chromosomes, several holes in her heart, pulmonary hypertension, and congestive heart failure, plus the expectancy of developmental delay. Her five older siblings welcomed her as the most precious gift. Those first days and first years were hard: full of doctor's visits, surgeries, and sleepless nights. But they were full of something else, something that kept my heart growing as if it were going to explode. I've always thought that the love between siblings is precious, and that one of the sweetest rewards as a parent is to see your kids love each other, but the love of her siblings for Paulina was out of this world. Two boys were born after her, who also adore her in the most fantastic way.

Having kids is hard. Your heart stops when they go through hardships; it breaks when theirs is wounded, and it tears apart with their pain. But, oh, it beams when they're happy, and it shines with every breath they take and grows and expands with each one of them. Your heart sings when you walk with your kids; it is overwhelmed with love—and with awe.

Last year, we added one more joy to our family: we now have a daughter-in-law. Haydn laughed when the ladies in the audience jumped from their seats, but I haven't only laughed having my eight children. I've grown. I've changed my plans to what I discovered later were better plans. I've been vulnerable to the limits. I've surrendered my will and given it to God. I've walked hand in hand with my husband, thinking we couldn't do it and then discovering we could.

Through it all, we discovered the meaning of love. And what a wonderful thing it is! It is so very much worth it, worth the pain and the struggles. I give thanks to God every day for trusting me with these treasures. I am blessed, and I am grateful.

Heather Salvador

Heather is a former U.S. Marine
and a homeschooling mother of 10.

When I reflect on my family, my mind tends to turn to life-defining moments. These are moments that most families tend to look back on with feelings of happiness and joy: weddings, graduations, the birth of a child. However, these moments could also be dolent. Perhaps it's losing a loved one, or a serious accident. Both good and bad life-defining moments are woven into the fabric of every family. These moments (both good and bad) have the potential to bond a family tightly together, and they also have the potential to bring a family closer to God.

My own family has experienced so many of these moments! We have loved and lost, but one particular moment has definitely perpetuated its effects more than others: the moment we welcomed our tenth child into our family.

On March 10, 2015, we were waiting with joyful anticipation for our tenth

child, a girl we had already named Rebekah Abigail. She was due on June 18, which was my paternal grandmother's birthday! However, this pregnancy was more complicated than the others, and Rebekah joined our family 15 weeks early at a mere 1 lb., 6 oz. This moment was both joyous and terrifying. We were not given great odds for her survival, and we knew the possible difficulties that could follow her very premature birth. However, we thanked God for her safe delivery, and prepared to walk the NICU journey holding tightly to each other, and drawing close to God.

Rebekah experienced a number of complications in the 108 days that she spent in the NICU, but she persevered, and was discharged on June 26, 2015. It was then that we faced a "wait and see" game. Would she reach expected milestones? What if she didn't? How would

this change our family?

June 26 was the day that most of her nine older siblings met her for the first time. Only our oldest child had ever been permitted in the NICU. This was the first glimpse that we had of the incredible blessing Rebekah would be to each of us, and just how blessed she is to have come into a family so large. We all treated her like blown glass. Everyone was so gentle with her, and so very attentive to her. There were 11 sets of ready and willing hands to do anything necessary for her.

As time went on, unfortunately, Rebekah started missing many milestones and it became evident that she had lasting effects from her premature birth and resulting complications. She is now six years old, and has been diagnosed with spastic quadriplegia cerebral palsy. "Bekah" cannot walk unassisted and she cannot speak. She needs help to do everything in life, and she will need care her entire life. This realization has brought with it so many emotions.

However, there has also been so much beauty, so much love, so much joy, and so much gratefulness. Having a child with special needs is humbling, but at the same time we feel so much pride. I am so very proud of how all ten of our children have stepped up in an extremely natural way to care for Bekah. They teach her so much, but they are also learning wisdom from her in ways that no teacher could ever impart. To watch this dynamic is nothing short of amazing. Do we feel sadness and loss? There are definitely moments these feelings creep in; however, they are dashed by the light that eternity allows us to glimpse. Bekah has taught us to see the world through a lens that we didn't know we had. She has increased our love, patience, courage, ambition, and empathy in a way only a differently abled life can.

Some people may think that being gifted with a child with special needs as your tenth child would be a burden. It isn't, and that thought is the very furthest from our minds. Rebekah is constantly surrounded by love, and she has a colossal team cheering her on continuously. Caring for others is such a huge blessing!

"Therefore encourage one another and build one another up, just as you are doing."
1 THESSALONIANS 5:11

Kathryn is the co-founder of Ignite Your Torch, along with her husband Joshua, and is the mother of six children

Catholicism. Large Family. Triplets. Priesthood. My husband Joshua and I both grew up as evangelical Protestants and never imagined any of these would be in our future. Yet we sought to follow God, whose "power at work within us is able to do far more abundantly than all that we ask or think" (Ephesians 3:20).

In seeking to follow him, Joshua answered a call to ordained ministry in the United Methodist Church. After less than two years of his being in this role, we came to a crossroads in our faith, and felt God leading us in a different direction. Joshua resigned, and we became members of the Catholic Church.

Along with becoming Catholic, we became open to life with a large family. God gave us a kickstart by blessing us with twins—not entirely a surprise, as I am a twin from a family where twins are more common than singletons.

As new Catholics and new parents, we wanted to live in a community where we would be surrounded by others who were open to new life from God. This desire led us to move sight unseen to Bremerton, Washington. After three years, we moved back east, near Greenville, South Carolina. Our family continued to grow, and we eventually purchased land and sought to settle down with our family of six. Little did we know what lay ahead…

In mid-2019, we found out I was pregnant with triplets. At the next appointment, we found out they were all girls! We named the girls Abigail, Chiara, and Bridget. Then tragedy struck. At the 20-week appointment, we found out Chiara had no

heartbeat, and that Abigail had Hypoplastic Left Heart Syndrome.

We had never lost a child and were hit hard by Chiara's loss. At the same time, we were confronted with the reality that Abigail's condition had no cure. Short of a miracle, the best we could hope for was that a series of surgeries during her infancy could extend her life into her teens or twenties. The surgeries required us to temporarily relocate to Charleston, South Carolina, three hours away. Yet, despite prayers and doctors' best efforts, Abigail died, at six days old, during her first surgery. The loss of Abigail broke us. Yet, in our brokenness, God slowly revealed to Joshua a new calling: the Catholic priesthood. Because he had formerly been a Prot-

estant minister, he received special permission from the Vatican to begin formation for the Catholic priesthood in the Ordinariate of the Chair of St. Peter. We do not believe this would have come about without Abigail and Chiara's prayers.

God has willed for us the cross of physical separation from our babies in this life. It is a difficult cross that we seek to accept daily. Yet it is only through the cross that there can be a resurrection, that eternal life where we will once again be united with our little ones in Heaven. Until then, God has given us five beautiful children, the prayers of our daughters in Heaven, and a unique mission to carry out on this earth. We are blessed beyond measure!

"To him be glory in the church and in Christ Jesus to all generations, for ever and ever. Amen."

EPHESIANS 3:21

Mary Grimm

❧

Mary was a columnist for the San Diego Reader *for 18 years.*
She lives in La Mesa, California, with her husband Ernest and their 12 children.

Mount Laundry: it's my name for the four-foot-tall pile of clean clothes that rises up in our family room waiting for their delivery. It's a constant reminder of the life that happens within our walls. Lots of coming and going, jobs and sports, backyard play and artists at work—the laundry tells the story.

My husband and I married a year after we graduated college. We knew we wanted a gaggle of kids, but we never put a number on it. Our babies came fast. Four in four years, six in eight years. Twelve in 24 years. With every baby born, our hearts and their capacity for love expanded. Little people with a bit of him and a bit of me blended into a perfect new little soul for Jesus—is there anything more romantic?

A large family is a beautiful tangle of love relationships. Sister to sister, brother to brother, tiny toddler sister to six-foot-three-inch big brother: it's a crash course in relationships and personalities. And life is all about that—different personalities learning how to mesh with and love each other. Mothering a large family gives you an up-close study of the gifts and struggles, the joys and sorrows—multiplied!

A new baby is a gift for the whole family, especially teens and young adults. There is nothing quite as cute as a tall, strapping son cuddling and cooing with a baby. And the fastest way to pull a teen or young adult out of themselves is to place

an engaging little person in their lap and then watch the connection unfold. It's a gift for both baby and big sibling.

Motherhood has a way of molding you, chiseling you, and chipping away at your selfishness. My friend Deirdre and I decided we need to write a country music song called "Jesus the Sculptor." The chorus would be, "Chisel away, Jesus, chisel away." This life has a way of deepening your empathy, and making you realize you don't have all the answers. There is definite peace in letting go of thinking we are in control, and letting the ultimate Creator work His magic on our personhood. In a large family, there are so many opportunities to walk these paths of life, the joys and the sorrows, with your children.

Then there is the extra gift of special needs children. "I love you, Gus," calls out our 10-year-old special needs buddy as he watches his oldest brother head out.

"I love you, too, Tunes," Gus answers. (Our little man earned the nickname "Tunes" when he was a constantly singing three-year old.) And Gus isn't the only one who is told they are loved all day long. We all get that. Our little loving man is a lesson in pure love.

Our son is also a great teacher of simple joys. I never was one to decorate for every holiday until our little man came into our life. Holidays and their decorations are one of his greatest joys. Now we Grimms take drives just to hunt for holiday decorations! Our Tunes has taught us these simple, small acts of joy and love…small steps toward Heaven.

"Amen I say to you, unless you be converted,
and become as little children,
you shall not enter into the kingdom of heaven."

MATTHEW 18:3

Motherhood: all love begins and ends there.

— ROBERT BROWNING

Teresa Dodge

Teresa is a mother to five biological children, a part-time mom of two foster children, and a real estate agent. She lives in Northern Idaho.

I am a wife of 30 years, mother to five amazing children, part-time mother of two foster children, and a real estate agent who works hard to help families buy and sell homes and properties in North Idaho as they are looking to raise their children in a wholesome and faithful community.

One particular event that shaped the person that I am today happened 23 years ago. While pregnant with our fourth child, having lost her twin early on in the pregnancy, my appendix ruptured when I was 21 weeks pregnant and visiting family in California. My prognosis was not good; doctors had to operate to remove my appendix with our tiny little girl, still growing inside me, along for the wild ride. As soon as I could travel, we flew back to North Idaho and I became very sick with infection, and my body started going into labor, which caused a partial abruption. My

husband was at work and too far away to get back home in time, so I had to ride in the back of a police patrol car traveling at high speeds on the highway to my doctor's office. There, they transferred me into an ambulance and on to a high-risk hospital. For seven weeks I remained in the hospital; at 28 weeks' gestation, our little Emily Rose was born at two and a half pounds.

During this time, my husband was working in law enforcement on the graveyard shift, our three other children were under seven years old (and were very fragile after not having Mommy around for seven weeks), and our baby I could hold in the palm of my hand. It was a test of strength and faith! Our family lived moment to moment, day to day, and relied on God's constant presence in our lives. Baby Emily had to stay in the hospital for two months. But, as we have explained over the years, "We wouldn't be the family we are today had we not suffered through those difficult times." Thanks be to God, Emily grew to be a healthy and loving child with no long-term health issues from her premature birth.

Now fast forward 23 years later: three of our five are married and having babies of their own. We are the very proud and grateful grandparents to eleven precious grandchildren, two who went home to Heaven as little ones. As I have had the privilege to be here and hold these sweet babies in my arms, I am truly grateful to love each one of them and to be amazed at their uniqueness—and to witness our children as they become amazing parents. "My cup overflows!"

Being a mama is a challenging, taxing, never-ending job that requires a faithful trust in our Lord. It has chiseled me like nothing else could have. It is a job that is heartbreaking at times, but has so many spiritually fulfilling moments that I would not have changed my journey for anything.

Karen Kelly

*Karen lives in Santa Paula, California, with her husband, six children, and two dogs.
She is a licensed marriage and family therapist, with certifications as a filial play and
trauma therapist. She owns a practice in Ventura, California.*

I didn't grow up around kids. There were two of us, just my brother and myself. My parents' unhappy marriage and subsequent divorce left the two of them living in their own little worlds and the two of us on our own to make all sorts of unfortunate choices as we essentially raised ourselves. Some of those choices had lasting traumatic effects, sadly.

I should also mention that I was the adopted child in the family, a fact that my family usually didn't let me forget—especially given that I didn't look at all like my American parents, having been adopted from Beirut, Lebanon. The foundation was laid for abandonment issues and the dark began creeping in like a thief in the night.

The zero-to-five years are a critical development time for a child. This is when first relationships are developed. Through these first relationships, the child experiences being loved and is in turn able to love. When a secure attachment fails to be formed, the child can drift through life anchorless, always seeking permanence through connection, but finding it just out of reach. One significant component of a daughter's first relationship with her mother and a son's

*"We are always in a perpetual state
of being created and creating ourselves."*

– Daniel J. Siegel, MD

"Relationships are the agents of change
and the most powerful therapy is human love."

— BRUCE PERRY

first relationship with his father is the concept of motherhood or fatherhood. This concept takes root early in a child's psyche and if it is not solidly planted, may well impact the child's future ability to become truly "mother" or "father" to their own child.

When I was 12, I was asked by the neighbors to babysit their kids. I obliged but hated every moment of it. I deter-mined in my 12-year-old mind that I didn't like kids and they didn't like me. I didn't do any more babysitting until college, when a good friend asked me to watch her baby for a few hours. I had never held a baby before, much less cared for one. I clearly had no idea what I was doing, but the baby was forgiving and so was Mama when she returned. Again, my 18-year-old self reinforced the narrative

that I didn't like kids and they didn't like me. Was I even worthy of being liked by children? By anyone? My insecurities were firmly rooted by then.

Fast forward a couple of years. My then-fiancé and I were deep in the midst of marriage preparation. A dear old priest, a Jesuit by circumstance and a realist with a flair for pessimism, asked the dreaded question: "Have you thought about children?"

"Yes!" my fiancé said emphatically. "Since I'm the youngest of 14, I would like to have lots."

"Wait, what? No," I said. "I am not sure I want any."

Cue the struggle between what my Catholic faith informed me on such matters and what my very being was screaming: "Kids don't like you and you don't like kids. You aren't worthy of their love. You don't

have any concept of what 'mother' even means."

This very wise, always succinct and to-the-point priest looked at both of us in silence for a while and then said very simply, "Six is a good number." And that was that.

I remember thinking the day we were married that there was going to be no way to get out of this kid thing, but that surely God would give me some time to adequately prepare first and get my act together. Not so much. Eight days later, I was pregnant. Shock and insecurity were forefront, after denial. Multiple pregnancy tests later and it was confirmed in my mind: *Yep, this is happening.*

As I moved along in my pregnancy, side by side with other first-time-pregnant moms, I tried to say and feel the things they did. I compiled the images of these new moms and their babies in my mind like a Pinterest board, continuously scrolling through the images, desperately trying to find commonality between the expressions of their experiences and my own. They were seemingly so joyful and excited about this new experience, this new life forming inside them for the first time. I, however, spent most of my pregnancy floating outside myself, keenly aware of a huge disconnect between my experience and theirs. And the messages that were so familiar were living alongside me: I was unworthy of any child's love.

Baby number one came along in due time. I had no idea what I was doing. (But no first-time mom really does.) As I looked at my baby, I didn't feel the ethereal connection that I was sure my other mom friends felt. I only saw my lack, my unworthiness. My tendency has always been to think and do the opposite of what others advise; it's my rebellion against my unworthy self, as I see it more clearly now—a defense mechanism, really—an attempt to keep self intact.

"Breast is best," so I bottle fed.

"Cloth is the way to go," so I used Pampers.

"NFP means 'No Faith in Providence,'" so we used NFP.

"Moms of babies don't work outside the home," so I got a job.

And so on. The best defense is a good offense, or so they say; this strategy was certainly a distraction that kept me in the realm of my head (and not my heart), arguing with others over what seemed to be the controversial parenting issues of the day.

It also kept me from exposing the swirling madness in my heart and soul, the place where I held firmly to my belief that I was unlovable, unworthy, with minimal ability to connect.

And then IT happened again. I cried. Again. A little boy. And, oh my, was he a crazy little thing… a Houdini of sorts. Looking back on it, maybe he had ADHD. Or it might have been

the Diet Coke I would occasionally put in his bottles. I mean, I was drinking them and he wanted some. Way too messy to let him drink out of the can. (This was probably the first of many "Mother of the Year" awards I have won over my time as "mother.")

But I began to notice that every time I "allowed myself" to become pregnant again, a little bit of the darkness faded away and something different took its place. I wasn't sure what this new thing was yet, but it was there, inside, competing with the deep hole that pierced my very being.

As the years went by, I had more pregnancies and more babies. I did a lot of crying, mostly "crying inside." So much loss but so much joy mixed in. In all, I had six babies I was able to meet, and twelve I will meet someday.

And, with every pregnancy, every baby, every child, a ray of light broke through and began to fade the darkness inside me: maybe I was lovable and worthy after all. I learned to connect, through what were initially painful but necessary interactions with my children. As with anything, when

"History is not destiny. By making sense of your own story, you can be the kind of parent you want to be—regardless of how you were parented."
— DANIEL J. SIEGEL, MD

we engage in a task long enough, our ability and confidence grow. And mine did as well. I "showed up" for my kids. I was there trying in my far-less-than-perfect way, time and again, to connect, to be in relationship with them. And every moment of connection created sustainment and built attachment, slowly filling my dark gaps. The light was becoming stronger than the darkness.

My chosen profession is as a child therapist, helping parents learn how to attach and attune with their children. Imagine that! I couldn't have. My constant takeaway is that I have been presented with opportunities time and again over my lifetime to hear what I need to hear, and the message is clear every time. "He who has ears to hear, let him hear." I am always trying to "hear" what I need to when I enter into relationship with each family with whom I work, each connection I make in my professional and personal life.

Every moment of connection matters.

As Dr. Daniel Siegel says, "We are always in a perpetual state of being created and creating ourselves." He also says that our attachment history, stemming from the way were parented, does not define how we will be in relationship with our children. I have found this to be true. I have changed the trajectory laid out for me so long ago. I have rewritten my story.

The light is stronger than the darkness now, although some darkness will always remain. I continue to be created through connection—the connection between me and my children, the connection formed as helper to those I help, the connection between myself and my spouse. I know that I will never be whole while in this life. But the light inside of me contains at its very core the promise of complete connection when my eternal life begins: the hope that my complete self will intertwine in relationship with my yet-unmet children who have been immersed in the Light from their beginning.

Christina Deardurff

Christina is a magazine editor and the mother of 10 children.

"I could never do that."

This is often the reaction of women who hear that I have birthed and raised ten kids. I want to grasp them by the shoulders, look them in the eyes, and say, "Yes, you could."

It actually is hard at times. But most of the time, the wellsprings of love it taps within you buoy you through difficulties; and some of the time, it can be just plain fun.

A word about practicalities: financial considerations are often

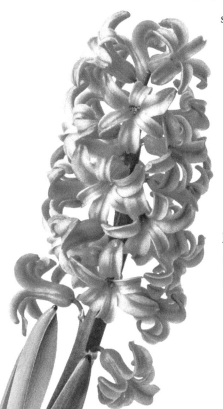

the first reason why a large family appears out of the question to many. To this I say, we raised our family on a shoestring, and the good news is: God really does provide!

We lived simply, but we also learned how to have a pleasant home, tasteful clothing, and interesting leisure activities while doing it. We found furniture at yard sales. I bought everyone's clothes—including designer labels!—at resale stores like Goodwill. We made state parks and local free festivals our weekend destinations. We drove older cars and learned how to maintain them. We enjoyed simple pleasures and found cheap fun, from thrift books and games to secondhand bikes to discarded backyard grills and firepits.

It was a lesson in detachment for me, but it was an even more profound lesson for my children. They learned to

share—bedrooms, closets, occasionally even beds—with graciousness (most of the time). They learned responsibility and self-confidence by helping to run the household.

They also learned to be self-sufficient. Teenagers all got jobs to afford things they wanted. They funded their own college educations and paid largely for their own weddings. They are now successful and independent in an age of entitlement and rootlessness.

And we all learned that a family is not about stuff…it is about love.

Krista Linden

Krista is the founder of Step-by-Step and the mother of seven daughters.

This is daughter #6, aka Mia.

I swore I'd never number my kids. I also swore that I'd be as "on top of it" with my youngest as I was with my older ones. Last month, after Mia:

- booked her own flight to Dallas,
- paid for it,
- made arrangements with a team mom to chaperone her,
- washed and packed all her gear,
- flew there and back,
- and got her own ride home…

…she gently reminded me, once again, that I've not accomplished my goal.

This has actually been Mia's whole life. And now her sisters are telling her she should be an engineer (even though she strongly dislikes math). However, she can solve any problem and is resourceful beyond words. After her graduation from engineering school, I will be one proud mom—knowing she has me to thank!

She also happens to be:

- super chill,
- has her dad's skin and long legs,
- does amazing hair and make-up,
- can pound the volleyball,
- and is stunningly beautiful.

"*By wisdom a house is built, and through understanding it is established; through knowledge its rooms are filled with rare and beautiful treasures.*"

PROVERBS 24:3-4

PART 2

Home: Where Our Stories Begin

"You too, my mother, read my rhymes,
For love of unforgotten times,
And you may chance to hear once more
The little feet along the floor."
- Robert Louis Stevenson

HOME.

I am in love with my home…including the mountains of clothes in the laundry room, the dirty dishes in the sink, and the ever-present pile of "stuff" that needs to be taken upstairs.

Our homes—whether big or small, new or old, in the country or right downtown—they are our launching pads and our landing strips.

Ours is a big 100-year-old home that has housed our family for the last 25 years, and other big families for generations before. Big homes are delightful, but also challenging. There is always room for one more child, but through the years it's been daunting trying to keep every room organized and clean.

Throughout our lives we all are seeking home, and someday there will be a never-ending, joyful family reunion in our eternal home.

"There are many rooms in my Father's mansion," said Jesus (John 14:2).

Home, no matter how it changes, is where we come from and where we are going.

And the ultimate reality is that, in families, we are all "walking each other home."

So, creating a home that is welcoming, peace-filled, nurturing, and thriving is an essential part of each of our life's mission.

May God bless all our homes. They are extensions of our mothering selves. And though our homes and our mothering selves be not perfect, we pray…

May our homes be places of welcome and refuge.
May they open their doors to comfort all, with kindness and harmony greeting each soul.
May peace reign, and God always be invited in.
May love in our homes quench every thirst and satisfy every hunger.
May home be a place where laughter, good food, and great thoughts
are freely shared and absorbed.
May babies always be welcomed and children always loved and parents always respected.
And may the grace of God permeate every inch,
from the piles of laundry
to the ever-lengthening family table.
May the words spoken and the words heard be life-giving and life-building,
love-laced and grace-filled.
May our journeys always lead us HOME.

They always looked back before turning the corner, for their mother was
always at the window to nod and smile, and wave her hand at them.
Somehow it seemed as if they couldn't have got through the day without
that, for whatever their mood might be, the last glimpse of that motherly
face was sure to affect them like sunshine.

— Louisa May Alcott

I remember my mother's prayers
and they have always followed me.
They have clung to me all my life.

— ABRAHAM LINCOLN

Catherine O'Brien

Catherine is a nature lover and hobby farmer,
and the mother of three daughters.

My husband, Joe, and I both grew up as one of nine kids. We met at Thomas Aquinas College, married, and have three girls, ages six, five, and two. We recently purchased a five-acre farm and couldn't be happier! Truly a dream come true for us, it's a blessing from God. Our pastures, gardens, and home provide our family with the freedom, beauty, and peace to prosper. Here we have the opportunity to work with our hands in the natural world and reap its benefits. We feel called to a Benedictine way of life—a life of balanced work and prayer, hospitality, and an intellectual and spiritual life enriched and grounded by a familiarity with the dirt and animals. Knowing cause and effect in nature is the foundation on which we can build a good life.

Cicero once said, "If you have a garden and a library, you have all you need." Aristotle might add some true friends to that equation, and Aquinas, the Eucharist. We choose all! Come on over and join us for a hearty meal, some live music, stimulating discussion, and a drink to warm the heart!

Fruitful and abundant blessings to you and yours!

Megan McDaniel

Megan is a social worker and the mother of six children.

As we grew our family through adoption, we realized that in a culture where blood is thicker than water, we needed to create a family motto, a manifesto of sorts about the activities, passions and priorities that connected all the McDaniels to each other. So, my husband and I set out to articulate what it meant to be a McDaniel. Our hope was that instead of honoring or delighting or commenting on the similarity between the eyes/height/hair of a child and parent (for example), we wanted our connections to be about attributes much deeper than outward distinctions.

We wanted to knit intimacy between kids and parents who enjoyed the same jokes, loved the same music, or delighted in reading, adventuring, or swimming in the cold ocean. We began to form a McDaniel culture, so that once we finished, printed,

and hung this sign on the wall, we had already transitioned our language in family conversations by adding, "McDaniels do second chances," and "McDaniels love Jesus."

The sign on the wall is now a reminder, though rarely looked at—because the truths and hopes declared upon it are lived loudly in our actions and words daily. We wanted the intrinsic truths of what it meant to be a McDaniel to take root deeply in our family culture, and they emerge beautifully in authentic, wholehearted connection and belonging.

14

*Maureen Ramos is a Navy wife who has been married for 35 years.
She has nine children and eight grandchildren.*

I believe dinner should be a dignified event. (Try that with seven children at the table!) Most people understand the rules of common etiquette: use your manners, say, "Please," and "Thank you," hold your utensils the right way, don't burp, etc. At our table, we have added a few more rules because I still insist that dinner remain dignified. Just because we are a large family does not mean we have given up and now raise

Neolithic humans. Over time, our added rules have come to include:

- No singing, humming, or foolishness at the table. This keeps the conversation focused.
- Stay in your box (those imaginary walls touching your shoulders and extending to the center of the table). This prevents reaching over another's plate and forces manners.
- No going under the table. If you do, others have permission to swing their legs and you may get hurt. This keeps the toddlers out from under the table and licking your knees.

"Strategic seating" is another important factor in keeping dinner time respectful. We have learned that you do not seat your dramatic child facing a window; they use it as a mirror to practice facial expressions. Do not seat siblings together who have a strong bond with each other; they will exclude the rest of the family by using their secret language. It is most helpful if the toddler sits next to Dad; Dad has a shorter tolerance for their tactics and they learn civility faster. Finally, the child assigned to "table" (setting and clearing) also must be the "waiter"; a large party needs someone assigned to get the salt, more water, etc.

A little bit of planning goes a long way in maintaining order!

15

Anna Skillman

Anna is a wife, mother, and home educator.
She and her husband have four sons and one daughter.

Do you have a behavior policy for church? Ours has always been, "If you are good during Mass, you get a donut." For years we followed this and it led to some good behavior, some bad behavior, and lots of boasting in the car on the way home (if you got a donut and other kids didn't). Some weeks only one kiddo earned a donut!

Then, one day, we were speaking with a very wise mom of slightly older kids and she told us their family policy was, "We all earn the donuts as a team!" After that, we made

church behavior a team effort. Now, if one person is having a hard time (of course babies and toddlers don't really count) and has to leave, or two kids are fighting or shoving, etc., the whole team loses a donut. This has really instilled a spirit of helping each other: the big kids learned to help the toddler with a quiet distraction, the little kids were spurred on by the "team" mentality, and we all started helping each other and working TOGETHER to earn a big donut treat on Sunday.

Some Sundays, we went home with no donuts, and those were great lessons on how we could help each other a little better next time. Yet, most weeks we all rejoiced with each other while eating our donuts, celebrating that we all got to enjoy and participate in church as a family unit.

16

Molly Valliant

Molly Valiant is a speech therapist and the mother of four.

The day I was invited to write this, I created a social media post comparing the size of newly sprouted lisianthus seedlings with a nickel that lay nearby. I am the quintessential watcher of the boiling pot ("a watched pot boils not") and tend to embrace this about myself. I check my seedlings daily, continually focused on their growth.

I grabbed the old nickel, placed it close to the little sprouted seed, and snapped several photos. Later, in the midst of reviewing, editing, and enlarging the photos, I noticed, "In God We Trust" shining in the background.

The moment provided a much-needed reminder that, ultimately, what happens to this seedling isn't up to me.

My thoughts on growing flowers and growing people are really very similar. In order to have beautiful flowers, suppress weeds, and manage pests, you must start with a decent soil—the foundation behind all possibilities. The need for a decent foundation extends to my family. As parents do, my husband and I continually try to cultivate this foundation.

Four years ago, we chose to move out of the city. The timing coincided with the birth of our fourth child. Our growing family needed room and we craved a community that we simply had not found in town. The move proved to provide a plentiful supply of both. We found a community of people who have truly embraced our family—a neighborhood where raising kids

is a responsibility for all. Our kids continue to have an involved, extended family, a faith background, and a school where they flourish. They know that, whatever happens, all of these parts of their world will support them in their growth.

We are setting their roots in the best soil we can create in the hope that these little humans can turn in to the most beautiful versions of themselves. We are not oblivious to the fact that there will be unforeseen weather and situations beyond our control, but for now we prepare, amend, and nurture because, as the nickel indicated, we place our confidence elsewhere and trust. "In God We Trust."

17

Yvonne DePaul

❧

*Yvonne DePaul is a parish minister, the mother of four children,
and the grandmother of 21.*

I was raised on the east side of Tacoma, Washington. We didn't have much money, but we had family. I was blessed to have more than 50 first cousins! We did not, and do not, all continue to live in the same town, but we share the same faith, values, love of food, and love of being part of family traditions.

The Catholic faith was the most indelible mark left on my soul by my family. I had role models on both sides of the family: parents, grandparents, aunts, un-

cles, and cousins who loved and lived their faith.

Growing up, I lived next to my grandparents until I married. Our extended family gathered on special holidays and holy days. We prayed together, ate, drank, and were merry. We played card games and listened to and made music all around the table. We all "brought something to the table." Sometimes it was a delicious dish to be eaten at dinner. Sometimes it was sharing a story. Sometimes it was leading a "Hail Mary" or relating a prayer intention, as part of the family rosary.

Now, our immediate family has a 21-year tradition of gathering in the snowy mountains of Leavenworth, Washington, around Christmas time, and 25 or more of us share an extra-large-size log cabin for a few days. We take turns cooking meals, play games, share the latest family news, and we laugh and cry.

We live in a culture not that does not make large family gatherings easy, let alone a large family sharing one meal every day. To be able to sit down to a shared meal, sometimes even home cooked, and talk to each other and look at each other and touch each other, seems to be a thing of the past. What memories are we building? What family stories and traditions are we treasuring? What values are we passing down? What religion are we practicing? What will our next generation hold sacred? Who or what is more important to us than our family? Let us keep asking ourselves and asking our culture these important questions.

Let us pray: *Heavenly Father, thank You for the gift of our family. Enlighten our hearts and minds that we may live more fully this vocation to love. Let our daily life and work reflect the self-giving love which You, O Father, eternally show with Your Son and the Holy Spirit. Let Your love be evident in the peace that reigns in our home and in the faith we profess and live. May our family always be a place of generosity, understanding, forgiveness, and joy. Kindly give us the wisdom and courage to be witnesses to Your eternal design for the family. Grant that the Holy Family of Nazareth may always guide our path to holiness as a family.*

Mothers can forgive anything! Tell me all, and be sure that I will never let you go, though the whole world should turn from you.

— LOUISA MAY ALCOTT

18

Annie Lockwood

❧

*Annie Lockwood runs companies in the timber industry and is a strategy consultant,
mountain climber, chef, writer, Ignatian retreat leader, and armchair theologian.
But, her favorite role by far has been Mom! Now that her children are grown,
she can be found writing her blog, "At the Table with Annie," playing her guitar,
reading theology, cultivating beauty, gardening, walking, and cooking dinner.*

I have long been fascinated by the setting of the family table, and how it is meant to nourish both body and soul, to bring Life. In our family, we hold fast to the tradition of dinner, but most especially of Sunday dinner, the celebratory feasting day. And this tradition, revered and cherished by my children, has brought much nourishment and elevation to our family life.

There is a generous bounty to God's table, and this generous bounty is the key to allowing us to love him with the whole of our hearts, to choose Life. Each Sunday, meant as the culmination of the Christian experience—day of feast and celebration following the Sabbath—as I set a beautiful table for my family to dine, I think about these words. I think too about the way in which the meal to come, well anticipated and cherished, will create in the hearts of those I love this same generous, bountiful life. Nourished by the time at table, the fellowship and the food, awakened to the Beautiful in all the accoutrements, plating, and service, how will their hearts be opened, and Life and *shalom* (wholeness) allowed to enter in?

To eat is something more than to maintain bodily functions. People may not understand what the "something more" is, but they nonetheless desire to celebrate it. They are actually hungry and thirsty for the "sacramental life." In our "eat on the run" culture of today, where we scarcely dine together at the table, we forfeit so much of the wisdom it offers. The young adult friends of my children like very much to receive an invitation to Sunday dinner, and often comment that they long for something they hadn't realized they had lost. In Welsh, there is a word that denotes this: *hiraeth*, a kind of yearning or homesickness for a home that never existed, or what C.S. Lewis calls "I know not what."

They long, instinctively, in their very souls, for this "something more." Yes, the food is good, the conversation enjoyable, and the setting beautiful, but the sum of the meal is more than its parts taken together. There is a sense of recovering something lost, or remembering something forgotten. For Augustine, to "remember" is to be saved. To remember is to "re-member," to live according to the wisdom woven into the order of creation. My children's adult friends are not wrong in their longing, nor far off the mark. We are created to experience this longing. It is meant to lead us to the Table.

The wise woman, as told in Proverbs 3, becomes the Tree of Life; she is the metaphorical Lady Wisdom who danced at creation. Lady Wisdom is the New Eve: she is Mary, who gives birth and understanding. It is she who sets the table and welcomes Life, in fact births it for her family, and in so doing, receives Christ as the honored Guest. A family that brims with life is a family for whom gathering around the table joyfully is a sacramental form of receiving grace—just as for the Church, its Eucharist is the means by which Grace is received. The life of the table is not an afterthought of family health; it is the foundation of its rootedness in Grace. And a family which reverences its own lady wisdom, and her sacred vocation, is blessed indeed.

Annie's daughter, Elizabeth Longwell — armchair philosopher, theologian, and student—contributed to this writing.

PART 3

Joy in the Chaos

I am NOT enough.

Everyone asks… "How can you do it all?"

One of the most freeing things I've learned along the way is, "I am not enough."

None of us are. And that knowledge has been one of the greatest gifts in my life. Perfection is NOT where it's at. We need to break open, like the seed, in order to give life. Perfection is closed; brokenness is open.

Oscar Wilde once said, "It is only through a broken heart that Christ can enter in." I believe this path of hearts breaking open, the "broken seed" path, is the mothering path. It's the path that leads to the sweet spot of new life and love.

Love is what Life is all about!

Deep, deep magic!

It's okay that we are not enough, because when we know that, and open our hearts and hands for help, God and others step in!

Kathryn Hederick, founder of Next Chapter, a nonprofit for mothers and children facing homelessness, said, "Mothers are the backbone of our families. When our mothers are lost, our children are lost, and our community as a whole suffers…we must stand together as mothers to support each other. This is the motiva-

tion that drove us to give birth to Next Chapter, a non-profit that provides shelter to pregnant women, single mothers, and their children as they address their barriers to permanent housing.

"Our journey in raising Next Chapter has often been messy, heart-wrenching and disappointing, but it's also been joyous, beautiful, and empowering—just like our own experiences as mothers. There is no one way to raise our children, just like there's no one way to help the mothers we serve. Everyone is an individual soul with complexities we might never fully under-

stand, but when we are able to remove stigmas and share the one thing we have in common—motherhood—we are no longer alone. Loneliness breaks our spirit and we become lost. Embracing our lives, opening our minds and being an honest, healthy, and positive support system for each other can and will make a difference."

Life is messy. Let's embrace the mess together, tackle our misgivings and see the joy that really does exist when we are no longer alone and lost.

God could not be everywhere, and therefore He made mothers.

— RUDYARD KIPLING

Monica Perry

Monica Perry lives with her husband in Vancouver, British Columbia, Canada. She was a columnist for The BC Catholic *for 10 years, and now works for the Archdiocese of Vancouver. She is the mother of six children.*

A story about my oldest son when he was in high school has become my "party piece." I tell it at the hint of an opening because I think it's funny:

"John Paul didn't do a lot of studying in high school," I usually begin, "but he had a really good time."

The fact that we christened the first of our six children for a man who would be so quickly canonized after his death will give you some idea of the naiveté with which my husband and I entered into this parenting business. Ah, young parents!

Our John Paul, like his namesake, Pope Saint John Paul II, was blessed by God with intelligence. Whether he would make use of it to pass his final exams in his senior year of high school was a question that worked my stomach into knots.

It was a continual source of surprise to me that I had given birth to a son like John. When I was in high school, I would not have been able to sleep at night if I had not done my homework. John Paul neglected to turn in assignments regularly, yet enjoyed the sleep of the just.

Advanced Placement (AP) Biology was the sticking point. On the bright and sunny afternoon on which my "party piece" tale took place, John was supposed to be in his room studying. That he was in his room, I knew. I could hear him moving around in there. But it wasn't long before he came out to answer the phone.

"That was Brendan," he announced as he appeared in the kitchen. "Can I go to his house to study biology?"

"John," I sighed, "I really don't think you are going to get any studying done if you go to Brendan's house."

"Well, I'm not going to get any studying done if I stay here," he replied. We both knew this was true. Didn't I say he was a smart boy?

Brendan was a good student. I hedged my bets and gave John Paul permission to go.

Half an hour later, I was heading out the door for a stress-relieving walk with the dog when Brendan's car pulled up. John jumped in the passenger seat and the two of them drove up the hill away from our house. I began my walk down the hill in the other direction.

An oddly familiar-looking young man was also walking down the hill about 30 yards in front of me. Both of us continued our steps until my analysis of this young man's receding figure and gait gave me confidence enough to call out, "Justin?"

Justin was my son John Paul's other, far-less studious, friend. He did not live in our neighborhood. That he should have chosen this moment to take a casual walk down our street seemed unlikely at best.

This boy's reputation preceded him. The three friends had surmised, and rightly so, that if I had happened to look out the window and see Justin in the car when Brendan pulled up, I would have known that their plans for the day were not remotely connected with studying biology. Brendan had therefore dropped Justin off at the bottom of the hill with the plan to

circle back and pick him up after he had picked up John Paul.

Discovered, but unruffled, Justin turned at my call. He responded brightly, as if surprised to see me. "Oh, hi, Mrs. Perry!"

The jig was up. Brendan did indeed circle back and pick up Justin, but he also dropped off a sheepish-looking John Paul. I am laughing as I write.

On the day of our marriage, my husband and I promised to "accept children lovingly from God." By making this promise we were, in effect, acknowledging that God had a plan for our lives. It was His plan. We were His assistants.

God's response to our affirmation of this truth was to send us as many children as He needed to reinforce the lesson and drive it home. Each of our six has provided a unique contribution towards this end.

John Paul has taught me to trust in God's plan. He has helped me discover that God's plan is broader, wiser, and, frankly, more entertaining than my own provincial preconceptions of how life ought to unfold.

"If you want to make God laugh," the saying goes, "tell Him your plans." It turns out that the incongruency between my plans and God's also makes me laugh.

God came to offer us abundant life. Making myself open to it has made me the life of the party.

20

Jacquie Banks

Jacquie is a proud mother of four children and 12 grandchildren.
She is a speaker, minister, and pastor's wife.

I struggled for many years wanting to be the perfect mother. Now I just want to pass on some wisdom to my children: you don't have to be perfect. Just be who God created you to be. I remember the day I discovered my mother was not perfect.

We were washing dishes—she washed, I rinsed and dried. We were talking when she handed me a glass that still had food on the rim. I was shocked! How could my perfect mother have missed washing the food off that glass? I remember that

she said, "We all make mistakes." However, that memory has stayed with me and whenever I am striving for perfection, my mind goes back to that day and I remember that glass.

When my children were little, I tried my very best to be the best Christian, best wife, and best mother. I even told them, "Mom is perfect." I can remember their little voices, saying, "Mom, you are perfect." My husband would just laugh to himself. When my oldest daughter was about eight, we were baking something—cookies, I think. I put the cookies in the

oven and forgot to set the timer. Well, a little while later, we smelled something burning.

I ran to the oven and took out the well-done, slightly burnt cookies (probably peanut butter, which were my favorite; later my children would tell me how not one of them ever liked peanut butter cookies!). When my daughter saw the cookies, she said, "Mom, you burned the cookies."

I remember saying, "We all make mistakes."

She replied, "Mom, you are not perfect, are you?"

To save face (I was probably about 28 years old and either naive or just not thinking things through in a lot of ways), I said, "I am probably as close to perfect as a person can be."

Wow, looking back, I can hardly believe I said that! Praise God for His Grace and mercy! This is the same daughter who shortly afterwards would tell me when she heard me singing, "Mom, you are on the wrong note." (Being the "perfect mother," it was hard to admit that my singing was off key.) I asked her if her dad sang on the wrong note too and she said, "Yes, he does." That made me feel better back then.

But I am so glad that I have a perfect and forgiving Heavenly Father who loves me in all of my imperfections.

Now my children are all grown and occasionally, when we gather, one of them will say, "You know, our mom is perfect," with a big grin and laughs from the rest. I still live each day trying to live the best I can for Christ—as a wife, as a mother, and now as a grandmother. But now I know that I can only walk in perfection and holiness when I follow in the footsteps of Jesus Christ. So, to my children and grandchildren: follow in the footsteps of Jesus—He is perfect!

And He has said to me, "My grace is sufficient for you, for power is perfected in weakness." Most gladly, therefore, I will rather boast about my weaknesses, so that the power of Christ may dwell in me.

2 CORINTHIANS 12:9

21

Teresa Zepeda

*Teresa Zepeda is a wife, mother of nine, and grandmother to seven (so far).
She is an author and a radio host, with a segment called "Faith and Feasts"
on Salt and Light Radio. She is the mother of six children.*

I took my last sip of coffee and jumped up from the kitchen table to begin my day's activities. In a graced moment I decided to sit back down. From my seat I could see my youngest, a toddler, in the family room. He was standing on the coffee table wearing only a diaper and a superhero's cape. He was swaying back and forth, wielding a plastic light saber in time to the music of Enya.

My eldest son, 18 years old, had recently left home to begin a job in a neighboring

state. My broken heart over that had not even begun to heal. With that in mind, I chose to relish the antics of my littlest one.

I remember when I became a mother in my twenties. I thought 18 years was forever. As other little ones followed, I wondered if I would ever get a full night's sleep. I craved escape from the raucous environment of nine children. The solitude of the bathroom was even disrupted with rapping at the door, and inquiring voices asking, "Mom, what are you doing in there?" as their little fingers wiggled underneath the door.

Even in times of actual silence, there was no peace. The lack of noise, I learned, meant trouble was afoot! Quiet triggered me into panicked action. If I did not act quickly, I was sure to come face to face with disaster…

disaster of the magnitude of, for example, finding everything and everyone in a bedroom covered in a thick layer of water-repelling Desitin. Every day I faced a mound of laundry that even my daily partnership with the washer and dryer could not level. Every doorknob I reached for left my hand sticky.

As new babies came along and the older children matured, the challenges of motherhood increased. I searched for wisdom when comforting a teen grieving over a lost friendship. I prayed for patience in dealing with another teen claiming I was ruining their life.

Then, I gained a new perspective. I had acquired the vision of one who has run the gauntlet, and in what seemed to me record time. I had the experience of one who has successfully nurtured a child to adulthood. The difficulties, disasters, and dramas that

came in rearing him now seemed to be of so little consequence. The fears and insecurities in which I had begun motherhood now were replaced with the assurance that I knew how to do this. I knew that I could make our way through turmoil and be able to look back from the vantage point of the other side. I had already witnessed 18 years of motherhood play out, and I made the conscious decision to linger a little longer in the joys it brought.

I thank God that I responded to that grace of quelling my industrious intentions in order to savor these joys. Although I still had eight children at home, mothering in my forties was so much easier and enjoyable with this new viewpoint.

My youngest is now approaching his eighteenth birthday. It is with some trepidation that I anticipate the fast-approaching day when he closes the door of our family home behind him for the last time. I will have the sweet memory of a diaper-clad toddler to act as a balm for my aching heart. But I will also have the knowledge that I had learned to appreciate and delight in those fleeting years of motherhood.

Rachel Daggett

Rachel Daggett is a full-time homeschooling mother of 12, and has been married to her husband, Jeremy, for 21 years. She and her family reside in Texas.

I am sure that if someone had told my 19-year-old self that by the age of 40 I would have 12 children, I would have laughed and said, "Well, who knows!" It was entirely possible to me, but also not something I was actually planning for my life. But here I am, living that reality now—and I wouldn't change a single day.

Having a large family is overwhelming. Every aspect is naturally bigger than average. I mean, let's be real, the LAUNDRY alone could send you straight to the crazy house. But it is also overwhelmingly beautiful in the most unexpected ways. I'd like to give you a glimpse of that from where I stand.

I have been abundantly blessed with nine healthy boys and two beautiful girls, and one baby that is yet to be born, over the last 21 years of my marriage. My husband and I were likeminded in our approach to receiving children. Our approach quite simply was: God gives the gift of life; we are here to accept His gifts. That sounds nice, right? And before you start "trying" to have children, you don't know how easily they may be given!

But once you have three under the age of three, or six under the age of nine, the niceness gets a little messy, messy like a toddler with a soft serve cone on a warm day. Don't misunderstand me; I have already said that I wouldn't change a single day, but that doesn't mean some of those days weren't the hardest I have ever survived, or that I always wake up smiling, ready to make pancakes and bacon at 6:00 a.m. for toddlers.

Nope, that's not my way. I have always loved babies, toddlers, and children. Does that make having a large family easy for me? No. Having a large family, like having any size family, is hard! That's because people aren't perfect and putting up with them is difficult, trying, frustrating, and... sanctifying, if you let it be so. And that, I believe, is one of the goals of family life, after all, to help each other get to Heaven.

So, practically speaking, what does that look like in a family of 14? Well, probably not like what you expect in some ways and just like it in others. Here are a couple of my experiences that put it in a nutshell.

I remember, years ago, after the birth of my fifth child, I was on a slow road to recovery and concerned that I didn't have enough help for the regular daily tasks in-

volved in feeding children and keeping the house running. My husband worked in our small family business at the time and didn't get to stay home with us for more than the weekends. The children were six, five, three, and one, plus my newborn.

I had gotten up when my husband left for work and moved myself and the baby to the recliner in the living room, not sure if I had the strength to make breakfast. My six-year-old came out and started putting the dishes in the dishwasher without being asked. I wouldn't have even thought he was able to do it. Then he proceeded to make oatmeal for his siblings, using the microwave on the counter.

After breakfast, he cleaned up the dishes and pulled the laundry out of the dryer and started a new load in the wash—all with very little direction from a tired, overwhelmed momma who just sat with her feet up nursing her new baby. It was in that moment I realized, *Everything is gonna be all right.* You see, he'd been learning how to help for years already; I just hadn't needed it yet so I didn't really notice. But when the time came, he was ready and willing to be all the help I needed, and that model has not changed as God has added new babies to our home almost every other year since. Everyone knows their own worth and how to help, because Momma can't do everything, but together we can do so much.

Fast forward to that same helper when he was entering his junior year of high school. There were now nine children in our home. Their ages were 16, 14, 13, 11, nine, seven, five, three, and almost two. For no reason that I could see, God hadn't given us another new baby on the same

schedule that we were accustomed to. The children had begun to notice. The questions started coming at regular intervals. "Mom, are you ever going to have another baby?"

"Mom, when are you going to get pregnant again?"

"Don't you want another baby?" and so on.

I would gently explain to each of them that I am not the Giver of life and am not trying to keep from having a baby. God just hasn't given us another yet. But the thing that makes this story stand out in my memory for ever is that one day my oldest came to me and said, "Mom, I only have one more year at home; I can't imagine it without a baby." My baby said that to me—my teenage baby. He just wanted another baby to love.

That one hit me straight in the heart. I couldn't have been more surprised or more proud of him in that moment than in any other moment in his life. He understood the value of one tiny baby. Priceless. I reminded him that God gets to decide, but that I was open to his timing.

Baby number 10 did arrive in July, before my senior started his last year of high school. And they were the best of buddies. He helped more than ever with changing diapers and getting Baby to sleep. He was always ready to take him when he came home from school, and nothing made him more happy than being able to love this baby. There is nothing that melts my heart like seeing my kids love each other.

I didn't know that love compounds exponentially. That has changed me, little by little, baby by baby. Seeing the way love multiples, it makes it easier to love more. I think love is meant to do that. Real love only grows, and in a big family, that love is overwhelming.

Mercy de Cordon

Mercy is a writer and mother of five. She and her family live in Guatemala.

As I write this, I am 51 years old, and I have five kids: four boys and a girl, ages 26, 24, 23, 21, and 17. I believe being a mother is a gift of God. My husband, Carlos, is an endocrine surgeon. Thank you, Carlos, for my five!

Maybe I could say that with the first two, I learned how to be a mother to the ones that followed. The first two helped me a lot; I didn't even teach my fourth how to ride a bike, or how to tie his shoelaces, because his siblings did!

The human heart is made to expand and fit many; there is room for everyone, a piece for each child. Sometimes a part of our heart will be happy and other times sad, depending on how the kids are, because they give life to the heart.

Having children fills your life! It is not living a life of your own only; it is enjoying seeing how they live theirs. I love parties, gatherings, and entertaining, I love having a good time. That passion spills over to how I parent my children. I want them to love their home and feel comfortable here. I would like to pass on the pleasure of inviting people and enjoying each other…to celebrate LIFE!

The life of a mother is like sitting down to eat a banquet every day: there's a starter, a main course, and dessert, and the children are in charge of preparing the menu. Many times, it is unbeatable, exquisite, but other times, the person in charge of dessert, for example, did not do very well. He needs to improve; he needs to correct. But other times there were problems getting the right ingredients, or it was done in a rush. But, even so, the good things are always appreciated. And those times when it was not so good? They simply provide opportunities to improve. That's the abundant life: to enjoy the daily banquet our children give us.

The mission of being a mother allows me to savor the experience of God the Father being with us. And, to the best of my ability, my goal in life is to ensure that each of my children reaches Heaven. Then I will feel that I did a good job: mission accomplished!

24

Anita Zepeda

❧

*Anita is the mother of 13 children and
is now enjoying the joys of grandparenting, as well!*

My husband Andy and I both come from large families; he has eight siblings and I have 16. We both wanted to have a large family of our own. This was definitely counter to the general culture, but for us it was an easy and natural choice. We had already experienced the happiness of growing up with many brothers and sisters and wanted that, God willing, for our own children.

However, I think the direct impetus to do the impractical thing—to marry soon after graduating college and start having children right way—was not from our parents but rather from a group of young married couples we knew who were slightly older than we were. They were all beautiful, fun people, living happily on a shoestring, so in love, and having the time of their lives with their babies. This is how we wanted

to live our newfound love: joyous and un-afraid of our fertility.

The genetic likelihood that we would be a very fertile couple did not daunt us, but we did not simply throw caution to the winds. "Plan" was not the operative word, but we did make some decisions about our future with an eye to the possibility of a mega-family. Andy chose law as a career over teaching. We decided we would, if possible, settle close to extended family. We learned about homeschooling so tuition for our tribe wouldn't kill us.

I may be giving the wrong impression by mentioning these considerations. There is ultimately nothing prudent or practical about the whole enterprise. That's the beauty of it! As my beloved brother-in-law, Pat, says, "It's a love gig." The world doesn't tell you that having a big community of love is fun. Children are endlessly entertaining, and when sorrows come, you have many to help you bear them.

We are grandparents now, many times over, and our youngest leaves for college soon. The house that was never quite big enough is now often pretty empty. But we stuff as many kids and grandkids in as we can for Christmas, and when they sing to us, it's a foretaste of Heaven. Since we have 13 children, Andy has come up with what I call the "King Lear Retirement Plan." We will let them draw straws to decide who gets to not host the aged parents for a month like everyone else. Since Andy doesn't have a retinue of knights, it should work.

I want a house with a crowded table
And a place by the fire for everyone.
Let us take on the world
While we're young and able
And bring us back together
When the day is done.

"The Crowded Table"
The Highwomen

25

Angela Lessard

Angela is an author, public policy expert, and mother of seven.

When I was a young college graduate working at a Washington, D.C. Catholic public policy think tank, I was called upon to write something on the twentieth anniversary of Humanae Vitae—Pope Paul VI's 1968 encyclical which rejected the morality of artificial contraception. I read the encyclical, then called my mother and father back in California from my office phone. It was a bit nervy back in the days of long-distance charges, but this was research! The fact is, I wasn't all that convinced by the argument put forward in the encyclical, but Mom and Dad, the parents of 17 children, were my experts. I got right to the point.

"Why did you have so many children?"

They were only a little taken aback. After all, as the parents of many, they had prepared many responses to this question. The responses varied to suit the situation,

from comical to slightly risqué to serious. I'm not sure they had ever heard the question from any of their own children, however. To us, the good of our own existence and even, most of the time, our siblings was self-evident.

But that wasn't quite my question. I wanted to know what specifically their motivation had been to forego artificial birth control or even the rhythm method to limit the number of their children. Their answer was, though, mostly in terms of following the Catholic Church's teaching in its conclusion about birth control. Still I pushed.

"But were you convinced by the argument that we can't separate the means from the end?" My mom rarely got a word in edgewise around my dad and the rest of us, and I think she quickly found an excuse to go practice her vocation rather than defend it. But my father stayed on to discuss the merits of that argument, to defend his reliance on Providence, and to make sure that D.C. life wasn't weakening my faith. Still, I remained a bit unsatisfied. It's not that I did not want a big family—as the eleventh of those 17, I only knew how to be part of a big family. I just wanted to understand the reason why Catholics should be opposed to artificial birth control.

I shared my thoughts with my wise older sister, who was herself already the mother of many. To my surprise, she recommended a book by Mary Pride, a convert to evangelical Protestantism from liberal atheism. Her basic argument—that women had been sold a bill of goods, coaxed into giving up their fertility to become cogs in an ever-growing economy, that fertility and children are a blessing from God, not a burden to be managed—resonated with me. The arguments about means and ends may well be solid, I thought, but what really felt like the Catholic, thoroughly converted position was this: God has a plan for our life, and a number of children he wants to send us. Who are we to say no to His blessings?

In fact, this inspiration from Mary Pride was not far from describing big family life as my parents lived it. Each child was viewed as a blessing, and each of us was cherished in our individuality. I think the evidence of this is that all of their children stayed in the Catholic Church, and all were open to God's plan for their fertility. (My mom is one of the contributors to this book—you can see where she boasts about her 300+ descendants!)

I was ready to take all the children God was ready to give me. All that was needed, then, was to find a man brave enough to take on a woman brave enough to take children as they came. The number of siblings I have usually came up on first dates, thus separating the wheat from the chaff. I learned later that at least one of my boy-

friends backed out for just that reason. My husband, Alex, though one of only two children, was undaunted. Yes, he was a committed Catholic, but he was also from a large extended family. His mom had grown up in a family of 14, the offspring of "passionate Congregationalists."

Alex had the experience and the imagination to see big family life as desirable.

Maybe, as an adoptee, he was eager for the blood connections he had lacked growing up. Together we welcomed nine children, and so far, two sons-in-law and three granddaughters.

Life has not always been easy: financial challenges and health issues have darkened some days. But I have viewed my marriage and family as a sort of magical prism that magnifies and beautifies the good in our lives, and minimizes the bad nearly to the vanishing point.

Occasionally, back when I was in the midst of the craziest days—when I was pregnant, nursing, homeschooling, and driving older kids to a school 20 miles from home—I would have to remind myself that I was living my dream job. Or rather, I had to remind myself to let my kids know that I never really forgot it, but due to my lack of virtue, it didn't always show.

Now, when I only have two under my care, and the youngest is 13, I truly miss the days of chaos—maybe that's that magical prism at work. I watch with delight as my daughters provide for their children the sort of home their dad and I provided for them: one of peace, beauty, order, and prayer. I enjoy the camaraderie and goodwill of my grown and not-quite-grown children. And, I remember that these days are also good, and that the Lord has blessed me greatly.

26

Monica de Zimeri

Monica lives in Guatemala, where she is loving every minute
of raising her three sons and one daughter.

My name is Monica de Zimeri, and I'm a 51-year-old Guatemalan mom. I have been married to a wonderful husband and dad for 30 years now and we have four children: Gerado (28), Herman (26), Alvaro (24), and Leah (20).

As I tried to recall some of the unforgettable memories of having many small children at the same time, one of them brought a big smile to my face. One night, I woke up to feed baby Alvaro and I saw some light coming from underneath my door, so I went to check on the boys as the light was coming from their room. I couldn't believe my eyes as I saw Herman sucking on his thumb and sleeping only in his pajama shirt, naked from

the bottom down, and Gerardo sleeping by his side, wearing Herman's pajama bottom (which looked like shorts) as he had wet his pajamas and his bed.

Gerardo must have thought he could handle things and that he shouldn't wake

up Mommy, although that meant leaving his poor brother naked in the coldness of the night. So, there I was, laughing at 2:00 a.m., putting a warm pajama bottom on Herman and cuddling him and his clever brother with a blanket. I went back to my room with a big smile and the next day I was laughing as I told the story to my husband and Julia, our nanny.

Being a young mother of only boys at that time was tiring, but every night's tiredness was forgotten with hearing their sweet voices tell me how much they loved me, especially my youngest boy, Alvaro, who said it all the time—along with a kiss. Those years drifted by too soon, but left us with lots of great experiences and stories just like this one.

Little did I know at that time that I was going to be rewarded with a daughter for whom I can't thank God enough, but of course, I am deeply thankful for all of them!

27

Leslie Wulfekuhle

Leslie is a mother of seven and a registered nurse.
She and her husband have been married for 30 years.

I am a 51-year-old mother of seven and mother-in-law of one. If you'd asked my 21-year-old self how many children I planned to have, I may have said four. Now, 30 crazy years later, I have birthed seven wonderful children, and have the privilege to call an eighth my son-in-law.

Looking back, there are many funny, heartwarming, and difficult stories to relate. The one that immediately comes to mind is the reaction of friends, family, and even strangers when they discovered

I was expecting a(nother) child.

With my first child, strangers would ask, "Is this your first?" and then proceed to tell me all the horrific stories they knew regarding pregnancy, labor, and delivery. When I was expecting my second child, I received good wishes and a hope that it would be a boy, thus "completing my family," as I already had a daughter. Apparently, in their minds, that was achieving the dream all mothers possessed: one boy and one girl. My third and fourth pregnancies raised eyebrows, as definitely my dreams were exceeding the average.

By the time I got to my fifth pregnancy, the reactions changed in tenor and well-meaning friends, family, and even strangers started to respond to the news with comments such as, "Don't you know what causes that?" At first, I was insulted, and I allowed their comments to affect me.

Then, I saw an opportunity to lighten the mood and came back with snarky comments of my own. My two favorites became, "Yes, and we are obviously very good at it!" and, "We are single-handedly saving the Social Security program."

Being a mother to many is not for the faint of heart, but I took courage and grace from God our Father, and Mother Mary, and wouldn't change a thing!

Children are the living messages we send to a time we will not see.

— JOHN F. KENNEDY, 35TH PRESIDENT OF THE UNITED STATES

Maria Isabel de del Cid

Maria was born and raised in Guatemala City, Guatemala.
She is a graphic designer, mother to four daughters, and grandmother of one.

I am Maria Isabel; I am 52 years old. My husband, Mayo, and I are the parents of four (actually, five now: four daughters and our son-in-law): Maree and Sebastian (Sebas), Alejandra, Isabel, and Maria. Both my husband and I come from large families and when we got married 28 years ago, we wished for a big family of our own. We were blessed with four beautiful daughters!

We planned out the wedding of Marcela and Sebas with great enthusiasm and joy, which was to be held on March 28, 2020. Due to the COVID pandemic, the wedding was canceled, but for Marcela and Sebas, their objective was simply to be married—and the wedding celebration, for which so much time and effort had been taken from them both, came in second place. On April 4th of that year, they were married, thank God, and were excited to start their new family. Today, almost one year later, we are grandparents to Tiago, and the family continues to grow!

In our family we have learned to enjoy life as God has planned for us—and we always try to look at the positive side of things!

Tracy Smith

Tracy is a mother of five, an ASL interpreter, and a teacher.

We had five children in seven and a half years, so there were times I would head to Costco with all in tow. Given I was wildly outnumbered, and they were young, I needed to make sure all were safe within my gaze and grasp, and that our adventure was a comedy rather than a calamity. We would pull into the parking spot, and I would playfully say to them, every time, "How do we act when we are in Costco?"

And they, in unison, would yell, "LIKE CRAZY MONKEYS!"

I would look back at them in their sea of car seats and booster seats, smile, and say, "Perfect!" Then, we would caravan in.

They knew that they were very loved and

that my intent was to keep them safe. So, this became a fun way to remind them that they needed to stay close to me and the cart, and not run off. Humor can be a wonderful tool for engaging children—and why not have fun if we can? This exercise was one mechanism I used to be proactive and set them up for success as we ventured about.

I also tried to prepare them for when things don't go smoothly. Children will experience adversity. Maybe it is a toy they cannot manipulate as they would like to at the ripe old age of 18 months, and the parent eases their frustration by teaching them how to articulate, "Help, I need help." Or, perhaps it is something that comes their way in the greater world that throws them off balance and requires a deeper kind of support. When a child encounters adversity, the gift the parent possesses is being able to walk with their child, cultivating skills in thinking and problem solving, resourcefulness, and resilience. These moments are nothing to fear! I found, on most days, that there is much a parent can do to be proactive and create contexts in which the child grows in self-efficiency, instead of experiencing unnecessary frustration.

Humor, love, gentleness, kindness, and hugs—interwoven with tasks which allow them to see themselves growing in competence and autonomy—lead to secure, grounded children.

I could write for days, as I have loved every minute with our five and continue to do so. They are the greatest gifts and blessings, and we all know the degree of effort that we as parents exert. I learn every day!

I would say that, no matter their age, may we only expect of them what they are developmentally ready to be and do. May we sit with them and listen. They think about much more than they show or say. May we just love them and let them come home from their days and rest and find security, so they can keep thriving and learning in the greater contexts of their lives. May we be love, so they know love, and they become love in the world.

30

Carroll A. Rodriguez

🌿

Carroll is a wife and mother (of eight), and now a grandmother. She is the president of Intitutio Fe y Libertad (Faith and Freedom Institute).

"How do you manage?" is frequently asked of large families, and then, in the same breath, the person invariably rattles off any number of plausible answers: military-style rule, impeccable scheduling, loads of patience, or serene dispositions.

Before my husband of 34 years and I embarked on this adventure, we, too, may have considered large families to be somewhat chaotic. And, yes, in our own fami-

ly, some days just flew by, leaving behind a blur of baptisms, First Communions, graduations, and other memorable events,

amidst the more routine happenings of our daily lives.

More than three decades later, after ten pregnancies, eight live births, three weddings, and five grandchildren, perhaps I have an answer: *Let go, and let God.*

"Learn to love the mess!" I once read on a refrigerator magnet, and this motto comforted me for a while. However, these words could be interpreted to mean that a better housewife and mother could enforce a better, more precisely engineered master plan. It would be peaceful and orderly, marching along at a pleasant rhythm, despite everyone's busy comings and goings. With time, I gave up that motto, when I discarded the illusion of control. I became mindful of God's presence in our midst. God, and our respective guardian angels, have always been in charge. Sometimes,

His plans are inscrutable and not at all what one would have proposed for oneself, but they are always for the best.

Relieved of my duty as the "omniscient controller," I was free to offer guidance, love, moral support, and many prayers. As parents, we learned to teach personal responsibility with freedom. Our family is a community of immensely valuable, unique, talented individuals. Each child is a universe unto himself or herself. Each person can, at one point or another, be a teacher or mentor to another family member, and, together, we are hopefully helping each other find and fulfill our singular vocation on earth.

And, there is so much more joy to look forward to! More weddings, more grandchildren—and who knows what else God has in store for us? I cannot stop thanking God for His countless blessings!

31

Elizabeth Forrester

Elizabeth Forrester is living in England, raising her family of nine children.
She particularly enjoys riding her bicycle through the English countryside .

Michael and I have nine children, and two more in Heaven. It's impressive, I'll have you know, because for six months of every one of those pregnancies, all I wanted was to be dead. I vomited all day long—even in my sleep. My mouth would fill constantly with spit. The nausea was completely debilitating. After having starved for most of the pregnancy, I would get huge, by which I mean, I packed on the poundage. Not cool.

My babies, however, like all children, are miracles of love; I can't imagine not having them in my life. Also, I'm hoping for a big, shiny, jewel-studded crown when I get to Heaven! (Not that it's about how many children one has.) But I'm putting my trust in God, and this is what I've been dealt thus far. God is pretty creative that way.

Though my parents are both from very large families (by which I mean epically enormous), I have but two brothers [sad face]. We were an eency-weency, teeny-weeny family by comparison. (I mean, my own big family of nine is "peanuts" where I come from.) I grew up seeing up close via my grandparents and aunts and uncles that not only is having a big brood of kids possible, but that it's a wonderful, rich life, full of love and laughter and joy.

As a girl, I was jealous of my cousins who had 10 or more siblings; to me, their life was magical. And I naturally wanted that for my own children. I wanted them to have the siblings that I had always wanted; I wanted them to have that rich, magical childhood full of life and love that I had only dreamed of. There is a payoff, mind you, which of course little Elizabeth didn't take into much consideration: the self-sacrifice of the mamas and the daddies. Particularly the mamas!

Childhood is wonderfully devoid of worry, isn't it? Grown-up Lizzy really wasn't thinking the whole thing through. She discovered the hard way that her own childhood left her somewhat ill-equipped to face the day-to-day slog of rearing and caring for nine children. In becoming the mother of a large family, I have been stretched in ways I didn't think possible.

I'm not going to sugar coat this. It is hard. Really hard. On top of the normal challenges, I have difficult pregnancies and

I live in a foreign country away from parents, family, and countrymen. (Oh, how I have missed American customer service and efficiency. And corn tortillas.) Living away from the motherland when trying to mother, not being able to share one's life with the people I care most about, is deeply lonely and an added strain. So, there's been that.

But, being a mother to my big brood really has been all those things I longed for in my childhood. It has been exciting and wonderful and full and magical. There is just so much love. So much grace. And I have grown soooooooooooo much. And I don't just mean my girth. I am a better person. Yes, I can say that. I have more compassion, more humility, and more wisdom. That, of course, isn't saying very much, but we're all on a journey, and God certainly is using the motherhood of my nine to bring me closer to Him, however far I yet may be.

I fell pretty madly in love with my fabulous husband when I was in my late teens. He is a spectacularly wonderful person. No, really. And he's still got it. He totally does it for me. And also he is the best daddy in the whole wide world. He is very involved and present in our lives. He loves us. Basically, we're the best thing he's got going and he knows it.

More to the point, Michael is a holy, prayerful man. He is the strong spiritual leader of our family. I have to say: marrying a good man is Step One in embarking on creating a successful large brood and maintaining overall happiness and sanity!

32

Sheila McDonough

✧

Sheila is a mother to five children, and a registered nurse.

I have three girls and twin boys, who are currently 17 years old. I did not intentionally plan on having five children, though I would not change a thing! I always knew that I wanted to have a larger family, but thought, *Three to four children maximum.*

I only had one sibling growing up and longed for more. My first three children were beautiful girls, but I wanted to have a boy. In fact, I was determined to have a boy. I decided to try one more time and to my surprise, ended up pregnant with twin boys! When I stopped to think about it, I thought to myself, *How much difference would it make adding one or two more kids at this point?* (I do feel God played a little joke on me by giving me two!)

As much as I love and adore my children, times have not always been easy. After becoming pregnant with the twins, I almost immediately started having complications. This started a long road to their arrival and adventures to follow. Despite the best efforts of my doctors, the boys were born at 25 weeks and weighed less than two pounds each.

This was our introduction into the heart-wrenching world of the NICU. I pretty much lived there with the boys, except for the nights, when I had to take Ambien to get any kind of sleep, even if it was drug-induced. Taking Ambien was a suggestion from the NICU nurses. I am pretty sure they wanted me to sleep so they could get some peace from my incessant questions and monitoring! But they were my babies, and, as a nurse, I had to know what was going on with them—especially once they started to have problems.

My elder twin crashed first; his ventilator was almost at 100 percent capacity and still not breathing for him adequately, so the only hope was Dexamethasone. This is a medication that treats breathing problems but, I was told, frequently causes impaired cerebellum functioning. As scary as this decision was, I did not hesitate to approve it. He was given this with almost immediate improvement. I breathed a short-lived sigh of relief, but then the other shoe dropped: the other twin declined.

First, he needed a colostomy. After that procedure, we found out that he had a Grade II cranial bleed. I was told this should resolve on its own…but that did not happen. He ended up in surgery again, this time with a shunt placed in his head.

It never seemed to end; it was a harrowing roller coaster ride from January to May.

Not only was it hard watching my boys endure these challenges so early in life, but it was also hard to leave my girls! While I was at the hospital, my girls were farmed out to different families to watch over them while I was away. I remain grateful to this day for my wonderful friends and family who supported and helped us during this difficult time. While I was at the hospital, I lost out on time with my girls, my husband, and our pets. The hospital was my home and reality for several months, and every day was a challenge. In May, I finally had both twins home and my family was together!

Life lessons that I learned during these difficult months were grace, gratitude, and a reminder that I am not in control. During this time, I found that my faith grew stronger. These are lessons that I am reminded of daily. To this day, I am thankful that my boys not only survived, but also with minimal long-term health complications. I reflect on how precious life is and never take a single day for granted.

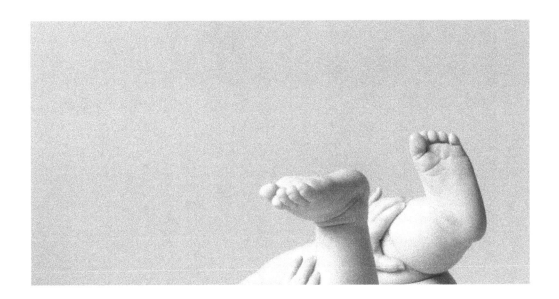

Children make your life important.

— ERMA BOMBECK, AMERICAN HUMORIST

Monique Patterson

Monique is the mother of nine children, ages four through 24.

This adventure has been full of joy, laughter, tears, and fears. Simply put, being a mother of nine is like walking around with all of your nerve endings raw and exposed: you are dealing with nine different personalities! Even without a corresponding college degree, you have been employed as the judge, jury, doctor, nurse, teacher, counselor…and best friend. Some days you hear a little voice that says, "Mommy, you're not my best friend anymore!" Exactly five minutes later, that same little voice says, "Mommy, I love you! Are you my best friend?"

It amazes me how the older kids help the littles out. For example, my youngest has his own language and all of the children are his in-terpreters. And, looking into my babies' eyes when they have figured out something on their own is priceless. You can see their wheels turning, so pure and innocent.

I have always wanted a big family. It's a hard job, and it's exhausting, but rewarding—all at the same time. Every day when I wake up, it's like I hit the winning jackpot numbers and we get to live a new adventure each day!

Motherhood is my life, my joy, my passion, and my greatest achievement.

Mothering beyond Biology

There are so many ways women can be mothers beyond their physical capacity to birth biological children. Some by their own choice, some because of circumstances outside their control, elect to mother children who are not their own—through fostering, adoption, teaching, mentoring, hospitality, and more.

In the grander scheme of things, we exercise our God-given mother's heart when we welcome our children's friends into our home, when we volunteer in a shelter for the poor or homeless, or when we share our spiritual journey with God with another person, and help them find their way to Him. This capacity to live in the grace of God's Spirit and to be a channel of that grace to others is an often unapplauded aspect of motherhood.

Early church history, in fact, records such women and calls them *ammas*, in the same way that the early church fathers (monks) were called *abbas*. These women were known for exercising a spiritual maturity on par with the spiritual paternity of the abbas, and were considered "midwives of wisdom."

"They were women capable of listening to the hearts of those around them in such a way that the Spirit birthed Christ in their

hearts and in their lives; and so they stood as midwives to that unfolding experience of an ever-fuller dimension of Christ living in the hearts of the women and the men whom they served and to whom they listened. The ammas had a profound sense of what it means to allow another to know the salvation of God." [1]

We celebrate all these different kinds of women who have beautifully broadened the definition and scope of "motherhood" in many diverse and impactful ways, and introduce you to a few of them here, in the following pages.

1 Forman, Mary. *Praying with the Desert Mothers.* Collegeville, MN: Liturgical Press, 2005.

Muji Kaiser

❧

*Muji is the founder of the Okaja Foundation
in Nigeria, and the mother of four children.*

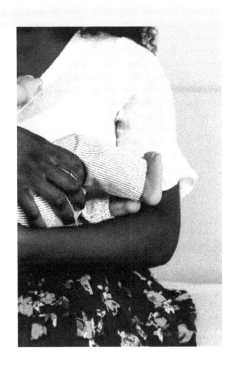

Mother. For much of my life, that word meant one thing and referred to one person: Maggie Okaja Mbu-Abang, the woman who gave birth to, loved, and raised me.

When I was three years old, in my home country of Nigeria, I fell suddenly ill. Local doctors were unable to diagnose the disease that left me unable to walk and our only hope was to seek treatment in America. Unfortunately, only my mother and I were granted travel visas, so my mother had to make what I imagine would be the most painful decision of her life—leaving my father, three older brothers, and the only life she had known.

Doctors in New York diagnosed me with osteomyelitis, a rare bone disease.

Soon after, they performed the surgery which saved my life. In recovery, my mother sat by my side, fervently praying.

After spending a year in recovery at the hospital, we were told that I would need to return for follow-up appointments every six months. We could not afford to travel from Nigeria to the U.S. this frequently, so my mother and I permanently relocated to the U.S. Years later, my brothers were granted visas and joined us. My mother started from scratch and built a beautiful life for us in this country. I am eternally grateful. As an adult, I would be presented with an opportunity to make a small sacrifice to help her. It was a decision that would change my life.

In 2015, when my mother called to tell me of her impending back surgery, I knew that I was being called home to help her. I moved from Hollywood, where I had a promising career as an assistant to an agent, to Ohio, where I began working for a non-profit clinic in Cleveland. I was happy to be reunited with my mother and was thankful for the year we spent together prior to her surgery. While she was in recovery, my siblings and I visited her daily at the rehab facility.

One evening, as I sat by her bedside, my mother told me that I was going to be a great wife and mother. I often wonder what inspired those beautiful words in that seemingly random moment. Regardless, they will forever bring me joy. The next evening, my mother passed away, as I stood by her side. As she laid in the hospital bed, slipping away, I recited the prayers she had taught me as a child. I cried.

My best friend was gone. She would never see me become a wife, or a mother. How would I know how to be those things without her guidance?

Over the next few years, I could feel my mother helping direct my path from Heaven. I imagined that she was praying to Jesus through Mary, asking her to lead me to a life of peace and joy. Her prayers were answered as I got married later that year and soon became pregnant. It broke my heart to think of having my first child without my mother present. Who would teach me how to be a mother? But, God, in His Divine Providence, brought me into a community full of devout and dedicated women, women who beautifully embrace their calling as mothers in a way that's rare in our modern, ultra-feminist society. My mother was gone, but I had been given the gift of being surrounded by and learning from the example of exceptional mothers who inspire and motivate me to grow in virtue, humility, and faith.

I gave birth to our daughter on May 13, 2017, during the 100th anniversary of our Lady of Fatima. We named her Maggie, after my late mother. Prior to her birth, I made the decision to resign from my position at a non-profit mental health clinic in order to be a stay-at-home mother. Not long after quitting that position, I received a call from my late father's sister, Reverend Sister Mary Rita Abang. Sister Rita and her religious order, the Handmaids of the Holy Child Jesus (HHCJ), founded and operated an orphanage in rural Nigeria called Divine Providence Home. The orphanage was located in an area severely impacted by the AIDS epidemic and had an overwhelming number of homeless children.

During our conversation, Sister Rita mentioned that the Nigerian government had discontinued the funding they had initially given the orphanage. They had about 50 children under their care and were in danger of having to close their doors, due to lack of financial support. I felt I was being called to use my professional experience in nonprofit management to help find support for the home. So, in 2017, I founded the Okaja Foundation, a nonprofit organization, in loving memory of my mother.

I often think about how those children lost their parents at such young ages and can't imagine what they must be going

through. Many of them have grown up without any memories of their parents. What must the word "mother" mean to them?

A few months after Maggie's birth, my husband, Nicholas, and I took her to Nigeria to meet my family and visit Divine Providence Home. Upon our arrival, the children greeted us with song, dance, and enthusiastically curious questions about America. I was amazed. Despite their grief, the children were filled with a contagious amount of joy. Their songs were full of praise and thanksgiving to God.

I held my daughter and watched as the children danced with infectious smiles on their faces. In that moment, I realized that their joy is a testament to the care, love, and faith-based guidance provided by the sisters. What did the word "mother" mean to these children? I can't presume to know. But, in Sister Rita and the rest of the sis-

ters who care for them, the children had been given spiritual mothers—mothers who, while not related by blood, were sent by God to nurture these young lives. The vows taken by these sisters means that they will never have biological children of their own. However, they have become spiritual mothers to many vulnerable souls who rely on their prayers, support, and love.

Many of the children at Divine Providence Home have been there since birth and will stay until adulthood. Over 140 children have been taken in since the home's founding. Occasionally, however, some children have been adopted into loving families. Often, the adoptive parents are couples who have had difficulty conceiving. Photos shared with me of the first meeting between the new parents and their child are moving. I am often captivated by the display of emotion on the mother's face and can only imagine the flood of emotions that must be overwhelming her. A mother longing for a child. A child in need of a mother. Brought together by God, in His Divine Providence.

For more information about the Okaja Foundation, please visit theokajafoundation.org.

Parents in big families are the happiest, or at least that's what a new Australian study says. The study, which was conducted by Dr. Bronwyn Harman at the Edith Cowan University, finds that parents with four or more kids are the happiest parents.

Why? Says Dr. Bronwyn, "We think it is because they purposely planned to have a large family, and while they report stressors such as chaos, noise, and financial difficulties, this is outweighed by the joy the family brings to the household."*

Cindy Frederick

*Cindy Frederick has four children with her husband, Dave. Over the course of 25 years,
they have welcomed more than a hundred young people into their home and lives.
They connect with these youth—usually from the streets—
through the organization called Coffee Oasis.*

Julie's mother died when she was a little girl. There is still some mystery about her mother's death; the assumption is that it was the result of a drug deal gone bad.

When I met Julie, she was hanging out at our teen drop-in time at The Coffee Oasis, a non-profit coffee shop that also serves as a base for outreach and resources to teens. She was about 12 years old at the time. As I sat and visited with her, I learned that she was not attending school.

She had been dismissed from school because she had head lice and had not been able to get it under control. She didn't have a mother and her father was a meth addict. That was the last year she attended school. She lived with her father and two brothers.

Time and space do not allow for me to relate the whole story, but God worked in amazing ways and her father was freed from his addiction during Julie's teenage years. Julie, however, fell into that destructive lifestyle herself. There were periods of time where she was clean and life was good, but they were followed by periods of time when addiction got the best of her.

One day Julie called me from the hospital. She had just given birth to a beautiful baby girl. Foolishly, she had used drugs prior

to the birth and the baby tested positive for those drugs. Child Protective Services was pursuing placing the baby in foster care. She told them about knowing us. They proposed that if Julie and her baby could come and live with us, they would not take the baby from her. We agreed and both mother and baby were released from the hospital to come and live with us.

Julie, a motherless mother, was in desperate need of someone to mother her…someone to say, "That's normal," or, "It's okay to let her cry," or, "You probably should call the doctor about this." She needed someone to give a hug, affirm, and be ready to lend a helping hand. I had the amazing privilege of being that person. She has a permanent place in my heart.

Motherhood has been challenging for Julie and for a while she did lose custody of her two children, but they are all back together now. Julie is pursuing her high school diploma through an adult education program and even stepped up to the challenge of schooling her children at home during the year of pandemic online schooling!

Grace E. Running-Nichols

Grace is a Fulbright scholar, educator, wife, mother of eight, grandmother of three, and a prolific painter of walls—in every hue imaginable! (She is also an author; her first published novel is entitled The Color of God.*) Grace lives in Northern Idaho with her family, where she mentors, writes, and tries to herd the various cats, dogs, and other denizens of their active household!*

"You're pregnant!" the bright-eyed nurse announced to my stunned, newly married self, as I held the emesis basin under my chin. "Let's call your husband!" she insisted.

"Me? You mean me?" I heard myself mumble.

From the office of his Army medical school, where he was a student, my energetic husband, Dennis, tried to hide his shock, saying, "Wa-wa-wonderful!"

At home that evening, staring over the dozen red roses Dennis had purchased with grocery money, we wondered if God had misplaced our five-year-plan. Dennis was studying to become a heart surgeon and, upon finishing my degree, I finally had my own Special Education class of speech-delayed toddlers I'd soon have to give up.

After our first-born son Gabriel, again God graciously whispered His own timeline into our surprised but thankful hearts with two more healthy babies—first Elias, then Magdalene, between our tours to Hawaii and Germany. But then one day, Dennis announced, "If I look at you, you're pregnant—so pray about

it and when you're ready, I'm having a vasectomy!" My heart stung. I believed God had a large family in mind for us, especially since He'd started us out early, so I began to pray about adoption. This time God's silence, and my husband's resistance, ruined my perfect plans yet again! One year of prayer became two and so on until finally my unfulfilled dream of one more baby (it felt extravagant to ask for more than just one) seemed like a stubborn longing I needed to squelch. But strange as it may seem, I was not released from that specific prayer.

One night, while we gathered before bed with our three children, Dennis said, "And Father, be with the child who is to be ours." We all looked up at him quizzically, but with sparkling eyes Dennis insisted, "It's time!" Yet again, on God's five-year plan, this time in reverse, we were given a precious newborn boy through adoption, exactly nine months later! Three years after the birth of our biracial son Malachi came our Latina daughter Salomé, then Zion, mostly Guatemalan, then our two from orphanages in Ethiopia: two-year-old Emmaus and Ezra Bethlehem, age one (none of whom are biological siblings). God had been preparing our hearts to adopt five children with one year of prayer preparation for each!

By the time we joyfully stood before the judge in Tacoma to finalize our last two adoptions, all through YWAM (Youth With A Mission), Dennis was 45 and I was 43. Our children's ages were: Gabriel (17), Elias (15), Magdalene (13), Malachi (7), Salomé (4), Emmaus (2), Zion (2), and Ezra (1). Across from the courthouse, at Denny's, we raised our pancake bites high in the air as a "cheers to God and family!" However, we knew already then, from the glances of fellow diners, that some might question the "family" piece.

A month or two later, after fielding awkward questions from strangers about our multi-ethnic, wide-age-ranged family, I asked God for a winsome way to protect our flock from harsh words. He gave me

a creative plan. With Dennis' blessing, I spent a boatload of money on clothing! I purchased jackets, hats, sweaters, pants, dresses, and even shoes in the latest matching shades from GAP and Old Navy—our children looked like stunning Benetton models (a European clothing store from my youth). On each outing I'd dress them in their new clothes and people would say things like: "How beautiful!" "Wow, you must be a family!" "These must be siblings!" "What an interesting family!" And our children would answer, "Yes!" with bright smiles or squeeze my hands. The big kids would affirmatively hug a toddler or two and sometimes even talk a bit about adoption in surprise settings. I knew that the ignorant comments (or thoughts) on the tip of a stranger's tongue, often unintentionally hurtful, needed a visual nudge in the right direction. And in this manner, God's redemptive work of forming a new family identity began from the outside in.

God has continued to generously provide Dennis and me with creative ways to raise our children, standing strong in a tumultuous world where sanctity of life

is questioned and adoption is difficult to understand. Through God's faithfulness and prayer, we are in awe that our family has now increased to sixteen, with in-law children added and three grandsons. Just as in our early days, our dreams and hopes rest securely on a timeline known only to God. With each new challenge, we trust Him to provide child-raising manna for the day in which we find ourselves. (Five teenagers at the moment keep us on our toes!) One thing is certain: each person, created in God's image, is beloved to Him and His plans are good. What a joy it is to be brothers and sisters in Christ! Together we are His family!

A mother understands what a child does not say.

— JEWISH PROVERB

Kari Lemmon

Kari is the mother of 17 children (ten through marriage and seven biological, two of which are in Heaven) and a grandmother of 10. She is a homeschooling mom, a devout Catholic, and resides in the Thomas Aquinas College community of Ventura County, California.

As I grew up between two sisters, my Christian family seemed larger than most. Still, I remember sitting in our Ford Expedition, thinking a bit wistfully that we had room for a few more kids! Not to mention, I thought, our household would be way more fun if it were just a little larger…

I believe these inspirations during my teenage years led me to want to have at least three to five children of my own. My parents were quite young when they began having kids, and I especially appreciated our youthful grandparents—hosting us for sleepovers at their house, helping my sisters and me with sports, and just being fun to be around. Little did I know our Lord had a different journey planned for me.

My twenties slipped by and so did my dream of marrying young. One by one, most of my childhood friends walked down the aisle; I remained the consummate bridesmaid. Most of the guys I dated were not the marrying type, but then I met someone who was Catholic. He helped me convert to Catholicism (something I NEVER thought I would do). We got engaged and talked about having kids. He convinced me to have a large family, perhaps eight or so, which was hard to wrap my brain around, seeing I was now in my early thirties. But God was slowly working on my heart and leading me to be open to life in an abundant way.

Eventually, we decided not to marry. While it was difficult feeling "all alone" as a Catholic, so to speak, I was confident God was still preparing my path. In my suburban Catholic church, there weren't really any bachelors, so I plugged myself into the young adult scene in the large diocese of Chicago. I travelled up to two hours to meet like-minded Catholics who could become friends or even a potential marriage partner.

Still, I wondered why God had given me this huge desire to marry and have kids… lots of kids… when it seemed it would never happen. Then I joined a Catholic online dating service, and a widower in California reached out to me. He posted pictures of his children, but only later did I learn he had *nine*; the youngest was only one when her mother passed away. It was the pictures of

the youngest that tugged at my heart as I thought, *She doesn't have a mother to love her and hold her, and she needs one.*

I remember having a "Maria" moment (as in *The Sound of Music*) after our first date, trying to remember all the children's names as I prayed for them after Mass. After initially forgetting the name of the youngest, I later recalled it and added to my prayers, "And God bless Sarah!"

And so, we began six months of long-distance dating. After the homeschooling co-op planned for the kids fell through, I offered to leave my job and move across the country to homeschool them. I had taught before, I reasoned; how hard could it be? It was not necessarily the best idea, it turned out—being homeschooled by your dad's girlfriend is not the same as being homeschooled by your mother! But it did allow me to see the dynamics of a large family, and I went on little "dates" with each child and got to know them. One thing I realized: the desire to mother many would be instantly fulfilled!

Many have said I was completely naïve for jumping into this challenging situation, and for trying to fill the shoes of a saintly mother. Looking back, I believe it was my naiveté that allowed me to say, "Yes," but also a belief that this was what God intended for me.

My relationships with each of our children are unique and special. I experienced a lot of growing pains as I became an instant parent to nine children ages five through 21, and I am still maturing in this role each day. If I didn't ask their mom for help almost daily, I don't think I'd be standing here today.

When we married, God also blessed us with a honeymoon baby—our first of seven (including two miscarriages). I believe having our own babies helped bring our family closer together, especially with my husband's idea of having the older children be the godparents to the "next set of kids," as he likes to refer to them.

Now I have 10 grandchildren, some the same age as my own children. One of my three sons-in-law calls my sons "bruncles" (for brother-uncles) to his own son because they are so close in age! And while I am sure it is a little weird for my step-daughters to have children the same age as their newer siblings, it brings a smile to my face. Life is messy sometimes, but oh, so joyous most of the time! How the God of the universe cares so much for me, that He fulfilled the desires of my heart in ways that I could never have imagined.

Over the years, one thing I've learned is to be willing to ask for help. In the beginning I tried to do it all, showing off my great culinary abilities… while pregnant. I was exhausted! Everyone was having fun except me, who was working away in the kitchen for several days… by myself! Now, I have each child help out making a different food, while I am responsible for the main dish. This includes the five-year-old as well as the 26-year-old. We love feasting together!

On Christmas, for instance, we have hors d'oeuvres, dinner, and dessert on the 24th, morning brunch on the 25th, and then hors d'oeuvres, dinner, and dessert on the night of the 25th. I make a list of all menu items, I buy everything, and then I have each child make two things according to their age and ability. I, of course, am still in the kitchen as part of the process, but it's fun having everybody pitching in and working together. Everyone also makes a different Christmas cookie, so we have a nice display of different treats. The kids sing and laugh a lot while doing this, and it is a joyous occasion!

Roxanna Ruiz Cabarruz de Florez

✿

Roxanna is an MD Psychiatrist, specializing in young children and adolescents. She is a Psychiatry and Behavioral Science professor at Universidad Fransisco Marroquin, the founder of the Department of Wellbeing at the same school, President of the Psychiatry Association of Guatemala, APSG and Central America and the Caribbean, and an honorific member of the World Psychiatric Association. She is a mother to one child and godmother to 23.

I come from a family of three kids. I have two brothers, and I am the only daughter. My dad is the youngest of five, and my mom is the youngest of 13. So, as it can be imagined, I grew up among numerous cousins; the street where we all played holds a precious and important place in my memory.

I got married young. I was in my fourth year of medical school and I'd dated Juan, my now husband, for seven years. He always supported my wish of having many kids. (I would say, "Eight," and he would say, "Four or six.")

But we didn't know God had other plans for us, and while my close friends were having growing families, we were praying to God with all our hearts that He would grant us the miracle we were hoping for—that He would allow us to become parents. I have to say I never lost hope, and seven years later we were expecting our first, Maria, and with her, the hope and joy that she would be the first of many. And with the years many came, in different ways; and now they are 23. That is, 23 godchildren.

Not too long ago, near a beautiful lake, walking and chatting with a dear friend, mother of many, I shared with her that every time I was at her house, I would be flooded with this immense joy, with the noise at the dinner table and the multiple voices calling her "Mom" many times in a day. She replied, "You know, your daughter Maria doesn't behave like an only child, because your and

Juan's hearts were always open to Love. You were always open to life, and that makes the difference. God gave you the miracle you asked, and made you a mother, and He also gave you an incredible husband, so that together you could radiate this love to the ones around you, especially with your profession. You might not have many kids, but you guide other families, marriages, and young people through your work."

I keep that day treasured in my heart, and every time I see Maria, I give infinite thanks to God for having entrusted Juan and me with this miracle in our lives, as well as the privilege to have 23 godchildren, whom we can love and guide on the road of life. It's a privilege we both embrace with humility, and one that enriches and fills us with joy.

This is what made me a mother of one, and also of many—my great big family.

There was never a child so lovely
but his mother was glad to get him to sleep.

– RALPH WALDO EMERSON

Nikki Shassere

Nikki is a writer and the adoptive mother of six children.

They each have a story.

The looks at the grocery store tell me the world sees a number. How I wish they would ask about their stories. "Six? Are they all yours?" I look at the children's faces— their miraculous faces, as they wait for their mother to respond. To defend our number. To defend their dignity. Oh, how I wish someone would ask about their stories.

We struggled with infertility. And then one day my husband got a call. There was a little girl who was about to turn eight and she needed a foster home. His office window faced her school. He'd likely seen her on the playground. But, after longing for a child, could we bear the heartbreak of bringing her home only to let her go? In a consoling voice, Jesus spoke to my heart

at Adoration, "My own mother gave me up for the world. Do not be afraid." That was our first daughter.

Our son was born seven months later. We met his birth parents a week before he was born. "A sword shall pierce your heart." His birth mother placed him in our arms in the ultimate act of love. United together, we continue to share his story.

Then, a miracle. After nearly a decade of infertility, our second daughter was born. It was a pregnancy with bed rest and hospital stays: "There's a 50/50 chance she's going to survive," they said.

Once again, I heard, "Do not be afraid." Her newly diagnosed special needs make the gift of her life even more special.

A call from my doctor sent us to the hospital immediately for the birth of our second son: "We need to deliver now," he said. A new little boy at Christmas. Our own holy night.

Wanted, he was so wanted. "Another one?" I heard repeated over and over when his little life was announced. Yet we grieved so when he was gone. As I held my Simon, born sleeping, I sobbed as I confessed to the attending nurse there had been a brief moment in his short life that I had worried. Worried about what others would think. Worried we would need a bigger van. Worried what the world would say. And now he was gone. To us, the number five didn't seem like a big number. Our hearts had room. I knew it meant more glances, more questions, more eyebrows raised. But to our family, he meant joy.

After Simon's death, a neighbor sent us a text message while we were on a needed family vacation. There was a double rainbow over our home. This, on Simon's original due date. God cannot be outdone in generosity.

Then, it was another day, having an ultrasound at the same office where I had last heard, "I can't find a heartbeat." I didn't want to look at it. While my husband held my hand, tears fell down my face as I feared the worst. All signs pointed to miscarriage.

"Look! You have to look!" The ultrasound tech squealed with excitement as she pointed to the little heartbeat…and then another… "Twins! Oh, you're having twins!"

Seven. We have seven. One is already Home.

Not just numbers. Marvelous, miraculous stories.

When the nomination of Justice (and mother of seven) Amy Coney Barrett was announced on TV, I pulled out my phone to spread the exciting news. While watching this historic moment, my thumbs started typing and I hit "post." Within a day, I watched as hundreds of mothers across America shared, "liked," and "loved," what I had posted—and felt deeply in my heart. We are connected by our stories. Not just numbers. Marvelous, miraculous stories.

She's likely received the same looks in the grocery store, been asked, "Are they ALL yours?" Heard the same intrusive adoption questions from strangers—often in front of her children. Googled

"vehicles that fit nine." Attended Mass in the vestibule with a wiggly toddler more times than she can count. Will never forget the ultrasounds and consultations with doctors. Defends the dignity of her child with special needs. Wonders how all the milk they just bought yesterday is gone. Seven. Yes, we too have seven.

The glass ceiling has been cracked before. But when Amy Coney Barrett's name was announced, it was personal. For my girls. For the wives of our sons. For me.

Amy Coney Barrett's nomination cracked a part of the glass ceiling not often talked about—one that is still looked down upon. And it was done with an army of little feet behind her.

As I watched her speech, overwhelmed with my own emotions, I couldn't help but wonder if she and Jesse were searching for matching shoes and socks for that little army before the military jet arrived in Indiana, as she patiently explained, "Kids, this is a very big day for Mom…"

Angel Nance

❧

Angel is a special needs foster parent
and a passionate creator of "home" for children.

My family doesn't look like most, and we do get a lot of looks when we are out in public. Just walking into a public building tends to make people do a double-take. Very few people around here have six kids, and our three teenage sons, one pre-teen daughter, and two eight-year-old boys, who are clearly not twins, would stand out even without the obvious physical differences.

I felt called to adopt from a young age. When I met my husband, I made sure that he was on board with this plan. We had three kids of our own before starting the adoption process. We brought home our son from Bulgaria when he was two years old, and although adding a child through an international adoption was quite an adjustment, it was also one of the biggest blessings to my family.

Several years went by, and I still yearned to add children to our family. After much prayer, my husband and I decided to become foster parents. Originally, we were going to only foster kids younger than our

youngest son, but then we provided respite for a teenager for a weekend. He became fast friends with our son, and when we heard that he and his younger brother needed a new foster home, we knew we had to step forward. While I had dreamed of adding a toddler, instead we added a 15-year-old and a seven-year-old to our crew.

Foster care is hard, but I have no doubt that this was God's plan. Whether the boys stay with us or return to their mom, I really don't know at this point. I do know that they are—and will always be—loved. I do know that I am continually amazed by and grateful for my wonderful husband, who has been such a rock for me and the kids. And I do know that I couldn't handle it all without God's help; He gives me peace within the chaos.

PART 5

Bursting at the Seams with Love

Let's be honest, people ask you crazy questions when you have a big family. I have been asked, in front of my little children, "How can you love all those children?"

To be transparent: I've asked myself this same question, time and again. I've worried and clenched my fists and let anxiety win, but then I've learned that when we trust, when we go from clenched fists of worry to an open hand of humility and receiving, God always shows up, He always fills us with His grace and love. Every. Single. Time.

It's as if He is Aladdin, holding out His hand to us, saying, "Do you trust Me?"—waiting for our "yes," our "fiat." And away we fly on the magic carpet ride of grace.

I always sit back in wonder as I watch love unfold…

Before the birth of my second child, Joseph, I anxiously wondered if I would be enough, if there would be enough love to go around. I loved my first baby, Catherine, so completely that I felt like I was bursting at the seams; how could I love anymore? Would there be enough love to go around?

That's when the magic happened…the deep, deep magic…God's magic.

When I looked into my second baby Joseph's eyes, my fears vanished. I instantly understood that love was not quantitative. It was not diminished by being shared. It grew; it actually multiplied when it was divided!

You can know something theoretically, but it is overwhelmingly powerful when you experience it. I saw and felt Infinite Love…It was staring right back at me in the blinking eyes of my baby; it was ricocheting between my husband, my two-year-old, my new baby, and myself. The love was not diminished but more abundant, palpable, warm, and even more dimensional…just kind of radiating… bursting at the seams.

My clenched fist opened up and I knew, "All would be well," and there would be more than enough love to go around. This same realization has happened with all nine of my babies. Kind of like the multiplication of the loaves—plenty to go around. And though there are days that I don't know how it's going to happen. I'm awed each and every time. There's always room for more love.

Love produces loves: the more you give, the more you have. Through the years, as I've welcomed each child, motherlove went from a solo in my heart, to a duet, to a polyphonic choir of many voices in one love. Love bursting at the seams… bursting into a symphony.

And, I've learned that, when I start to be anxious, and I know that I'm not enough, to just pause for a minute and listen and open my hands and my heart… and the music of Grace begins to play. I drink in the rich, dimensional tones of never-ending motherlove, drawn from the symphony of Infinite Love Himself.

God always comes to the rescue. Love always finds a way. Yes, we mothers of many burst at the seams…with Love.

41

Wendy-Irene Zepeda

Wendy-Irene is a wife, homeschooling mother of six, musician, and writer.

The tremendous strength of the feelings that come with motherhood probably surprises every new mother. A mother of many children discovers that with each child, those feelings blossom anew: overwhelming love, desire to protect, and joy in the simple existence of my child. With each baby, as a friend with nine said, "I fall in love all over again." Each child calls out a new delight in their own existence; they give me joy just by being, just by existing. That joy is so strong that even seeing a child who looks like mine makes me happy!

I also rejoice in even their smallest attempts to do things: the first stumbling steps, the first bumbling words, give a happiness disproportional to their face value. And, if those words or actions are oriented to me—if the baby is walking into my arms, or just barely managing to say in gibberish, "I love you"—well, those actions sink even more deeply into my heart, even if it's just the moment my baby first focuses his eyes enough to look into mine. That is a golden moment. One of the gifts of having many children is learning to recognize and savor these moments, as I realize more and more their importance and how quickly a child grows up.

This love and delight doesn't get spread more thinly over many children, but rather it is multiplied. Every now and then I wonder at the fact that I'm infinitely rich…

six times over. Each child has an immortal soul, is capable of receiving the infinite God into themselves; the treasures of each individual are unlimited. And I have six of these unlimited treasures.

One can't help wondering where all these powerful feelings came from. Where does this well of love have its source? It's both humbling and encouraging to realize that this love, this desire to protect, this joy in my child's existence, flows from and is a tiny reflection of how God feels about us. As a member of Christ's Body, I give Him joy just by being. When He sees me from Heaven, He sees someone who reminds Him of His beloved Son, in whom He is well pleased. And, my klutzy attempts to do good, my half-baked prayers and imperfect attempts at showing love, delight Him—rather like my baby's earnest attempts to give me a kiss or feed me a cracker do.

When I brought my last baby home, it was lovely to see each of her siblings hold her for the first time. The older ones had helped take care of me during her time in

the womb; the young ones had given her hugs and "kisses" while she was *in utero*. They'd all prayed for her, and now they held her in their arms with tender excitement. She didn't know what they'd done for her, and was barely aware they were holding her…but she was surrounded by love. And as she's grown, it's evident that the atmosphere of her siblings' love is like oxygen, strengthening and supporting her. Watching this relationship gives my husband and me such joy. It is a gift beyond words for parents to see their children love each other.

I find I better understand the Communion of Saints, that family of thousands, from watching my children. Don't get me wrong—my kids certainly have their times of friction! But still, they love each other so dearly and get their kicks out of each other. They have fun together, enjoy each other's accomplishments, help each other, and have a sense of belonging and context from one another.

How vivid this makes the love of the saints, our big brothers and sisters in Christ, for us little siblings! They work and pray for us while we are barely even aware of their existence, and hold us tenderly in their care. And how vivid it makes God's rejoicing, His profound satisfaction in seeing His little children love one another!

St. Paul famously said, "…the woman…will be saved by childbearing" (see 1 Timothy 2:15). I think one of the ways God wants me, this mother, this woman, to be "saved by childbearing" is by bringing me through the intense experience of the interplay of love in a big family to a deeper appreciation of His profound love for each member of His family, the Church, and of how He lets us participate in giving and receiving that Love.

42

Connie Ladenburg

Connie Ladenburg is a mother of five and grandmother of 11. After 25 years being home full-time raising her children, she earned Bachelor's and Master's degrees in social work and went on to serve on city and county councils, and in the Washington State Legislature.

Is there a right time to become a mother? And how much time should one spend in making that decision? For me, it was no time at all.

I was 19 when I found out I was pregnant. At first, my husband and I were shocked. We were both in college, with ideas about the future but no definite plans. This discovery changed all of that in a hurry. We decided that he would continue on in school, becoming a lawyer, and I would be a stay-at-home mom. Although I was a little bit afraid of motherhood, I also was very excited. But I was an anomaly in my peer group. While all of my friends were

finishing school and becoming "career" women, I was deciding to raise our son— and four more after that.

Having five children often raised eyebrows and sometimes frowns from people. When we would go to receptions or other social events, I was often ignored in conversations, most often by other women who apparently thought that because I spent my day working with my children instead of in an office, I had nothing of value to say. It took 10 to 15 years for that attitude to change when they were then having children and seeing the value that parenting has on children and, through that, on our community. That is what parenting is to me. Raising my five children was building a community—first, within our family, then our neighborhood and schools, and then in our community.

I was a stay-at-home mother for 25 years. During the next 25 years, I went back to school and earned Bachelor's and Master's degrees in Social Work. I worked with teens in substance abuse prevention work, ran for elected office, and served on the City Council, the State Legislature, and the County Council. My husband and I have now been married for 51 years. My time to start parenting was exactly the right time for me! I would not change one thing.

We have 11 grandchildren. I have always said that I measure my success as a parent when I see my children parent successfully. Our grandchildren are fabulous so I have to say that all of us have been successful at parenting!

43

Mary Gallagher Senecal

Mary is a mother of five (three sons, two daughters), and an oncology nurse. She has five grandchildren.

We are the Senecals. There are seven of us: Frank, my husband, myself, and our children: Owen, Conor, Maura, Clare, and Aidan. What follows is just one of the hundreds of stories, mostly humorous, that have occurred over the years.

In 1999, when Aidan, our youngest, was about five, we decided to take the whole family on a trip to Italy. Before we left, we told our kids about all the wonderful things Italy offers, including its rich history, beautiful scenery, and fantastic food—especially gelato.

We were excited to explore Rome, Florence, Assisi, and Cinque Terre. Rome was our first stop. We checked into a lovely hotel near the Trevi Fountain, where we needed two rooms, given our family's size. Our four oldest children would sleep in one room while Frank, Aidan, and I would sleep in another.

The next day was our first full day of sightseeing. We went for a walk after breakfast to orient ourselves with our surroundings. The cafes and people packed into the narrow streets were impressive. We found the Trevi Fountain and were awed by its statues and age. Afterwards, we strolled back to the hotel for a rest.

As soon as we got to our room, Frank and I noticed that Aidan wasn't with us, and we thought he must be in the second room with our other kids. We went to check after a short time had passed and discovered that

Aidan was in neither room—and nowhere to be found in the hotel.

In no time, we were out the front door and divided into two groups heading in different directions to look for him. It was a very tense 10 to 15 minutes. Finally, Owen spotted him in an ice cream shop. He was teary-eyed but being handed an ice cream cone. Apparently, he'd realized when he stopped to look in a window that he'd lost us, and quickly found a policeman. This gentleman did not speak English, but took him into the ice cream shop, where he knew the owner spoke English, telling her Aidan was lost and couldn't find his family. The shop owner was offering Aidan a cone and trying to get some more information when Owen spotted him. We soon all found each other again and were too glad to be reunited with Aidan.

This story has a very happy ending, and is a good illustration of how everyone working together can solve a problem. After this, we were always sure that everyone knew the name of the hotel, and we re-adopted the "buddy" system so that everyone was always accounted for. Having a large family has many joys, but also many challenges!

Youth fades; love droops;
the leaves of friendship fall;
a mother's secret hope outlives them all.

— OLIVER WENDELL HOLMES

44

Molly Smillie

Molly is a writer and the mother of nine children.

"No, you're not," my husband JJ said.

It was my 47th birthday. We had married off our eldest daughter two years earlier, and welcomed our first grandchild a year and a bit after that. Our youngest, at four and a half, had just landed his first job and moved out. (Okay, not really, but he definitely was sleeping in his own bed.) JJ and I, after 25 years of marriage, and 24 years of raising eight kids, were moving into a new phase: grandparenthood.

Sure, it was a little bittersweet to think that from now on, all the babies in the

family would belong to our kids, but everything has its time and now was the time for us to hand over the infant-care reins to the next generation. Or so we thought.

"Oh, yes, I am," I replied.

And indeed I was. *Pregnant.* God can be a pretty funny Guy sometimes, and this time the joke was on us. After the initial shock had passed, JJ rallied and gave me a hug. We'd been here before, and each time—though the timing might not have always seemed perfect, and though we knew there were some who would question our sanity—we had always welcomed the news with great joy. After all, what, really, could possibly be better than a new baby?!

I guess I shouldn't have been surprised by my pregnancy. I was born when my mother was 42, and my little sister came along five years later, when Mom was 47.

Mom said that was the shortest pregnancy she'd ever had (and it was her twelfth), because for the first five months she thought she was in menopause. It must have been quite a surprise when little Menopause started making her presence known. No, don't be ridiculous—they actually named her Elizabeth. By the way, Liz is now married to a guy who took great delight in remarking throughout my last pregnancy, "Grandma's havin' a baby!" every time he saw me. We love him dearly.

Planted in the house of the Lord
They will flourish in the court of our God,
Still bearing fruit when they are old,
Still full of sap, still green,
To proclaim that the Lord is just.
In Him, my Rock, there is no wrong.
PSALM 92:13-16

Twenty-five years is kind of a long span of childbearing, and it wasn't without its complicating factors. Every stage of parenthood has its challenges, of course, but I'm not sure I'd ever been stretched quite as far as I was when mothering babies and adult children at the same time. When, after losing sleep with a newborn and ushering various children through the day and finally collapsing into bed, the phone would ring just as my heavy head was dropping onto the pillow. A daughter away at college needed to talk to her mama, and it couldn't wait. Or, when I was planning a wedding while homeschooling and chasing a nursing toddler. And, it broke my heart to have to tell Tess we'd miss her college graduation because that's when the new baby was due.

But I'd be lying if I only told you the hard parts. Because, oh the joys! What could be better than a college student rushing in with tears in her eyes to embrace me and the months-old little brother that she's just meeting for the first time? Or the baby girl who won't be held by anyone but her 18-year-old brother? And I still remember the day I told Marie, herself a mother for the previous year, that she had another sibling on the way. You'd think I'd just given her a new car or a million dollars—such happiness and excitement! And then a few months later to find that we, mother and daughter, were both carrying babies—aunt and niece, as it turned out—well, what a blessing! God's generosity abounds!

Our youngest is now seven, and I'm in the throes of planning Ciara's wedding—number five, our delightful middle child. Chatting about wedding things with Marie over the phone the other day, she mused that perhaps one day we'll be planning our daughters' weddings together. What a lovely thought.

Children are the hands by which
we take hold of heaven.

— HENRY WARD BEECHER,

REVEREND AND SOCIAL ACTIVIST

45

Judy Manza

Judy Manza is a veteran, a teacher, and an advocate for the vulnerable.
She is the mother of six children.

I gave birth to my sixth child just a few weeks before my 44th birthday. The previous fall, my youngest child started first grade, marking the first time in 16 years that I did not have one or more children at home during the day. There were many activities with which I planned to fill my newly freed-up weekdays. Coping with pregnancy was definitely not one of them!

Yet, here I was in April, taking my six-day-old baby boy to Easter Mass with the rest of the family, and adjusting once more to the demands of an infant. The experience of having a "caboose baby" taught me many life lessons and brought unexpected joys.

The first lesson was humility. I could not help but be humbled, being mistaken for the baby's grandma instead of his mother, or—worse yet—having people assume my

teenage children were the baby's parents! When perfect strangers demanded to know if "these are all your children" and then stated, "You will never be able to afford them all," what else could I do but smile and humbly refrain from an unkind response?

The second lesson was serenity. At the time of our youngest child's birth, we had two children in high school, one in junior high, and two in grade school. Our family life was a whirlwind of school, homework, choir and band concerts, baseball games, and dance lessons. Into this chaotic schedule came a tiny baby pleading, just by his presence, for us to "slow down." And each one of us, at various times, managed to take time away from the fray just to hold the baby as he rested—and find peace in the stillness. Even the friends of our high-school-aged children would stop by after sports practices to spend time with the baby. The restorative nature of these serenity breaks cannot be overstated!

The third lesson was perspective. Having a child later in life provided me with the crucial life experience of recognizing what was important and what was not. It helped me take joy in the little things that I had sometimes overlooked as a young mother, when I was more focused on societal expectations of the next stage of my child's development, or how my child was faring on the growth charts. Experiencing and treasuring all the stages of childhood a sixth time was a gift I neither anticipated nor took for granted.

The fourth lesson was acceptance. By accepting God's plan for my life, even though it was not initially *my* plan, I became more open to the blessings God had in store for me. Without our "caboose baby," there are friends we would never have met and precious family memories that would not exist. We would not have had any of our children with us for the holidays during the pandemic years of 2020 and 2021—because child number six was still a member of our household, we could at least celebrate indoors with him! And my gray hair notwithstanding, he has kept me young at heart!

Susan Neyman

Susan is a teacher and the mother of four children.

"Blessed is the man whose quiver is full" (Psalm 127:5). The Jewish tradition defines a "quiver" as "full" with a boy and a girl. God granted my husband's and my quiver to be doubly full. Our arrows are a 30-year-old son, 28-year-old daughter, and twins: a boy and girl of 23.

I raised them on my knees in prayer. I felt all the pains, heartaches, and joys they felt as they were growing up. I rejoice in thanksgiving that they have grown to be men and women who love the Lord and contribute positively to the world around them.

I'm also thankful for the three additional arrows now added to our quiver, with two sons-in-law and a daughter-in-law. My heart expands even more with every addition! And as our home has emptied of our own children, grandchildren are starting to fill the gap. It gives me great joy to see my sons and daughters take parenting as a responsibility and gift to cherish, just as my husband and I did.

Once more, my heart expands in love with each new grandchild, and once more, I go to my knees, to pray for the safety and upbringing of my five grandchildren—and my future grandchildren. And, my husband and I pray that our house will always be a haven for a tired spirit, a place of meeting for merriment and celebration, and a home of rejoicing in a quiver bursting with love.

Angela Roessner

Angela is a teacher, and the mother of eight children.

"Mom, how do you catch a unique rabbit?" My newly dubbed "10-year-old" son asked, as he finished unwrapping his birthday gifts.

"I don't know, Alex. How do you do it?" I wondered. I truly did not know the answer to this simple joke because my brain had not been used to critical thinking. The survival mode had been fully engaged for a solid 13 years, and I had not been able to figure out even the easiest kid jokes.

"You 'neek up on it! Do you get it, Mom? Unique-up-on it?!" he repeated as he chuckled aloud. I did not know if uniqueness was a theme for all 10-year-old boys, but to me, it seemed appropriate. Neither were 10-year-olds "little boys" anymore, nor were they teens. I think this was the year a child officially became a "tween." Nevertheless, the word *unique* had me thinking about big family life.

Growing up, my religion teachers and parents told me that God made me unique. We were all created special and different because God had a unique plan for each of us. Psalm 139 reminded me, "You formed my inward parts; you knit me together in my mother's womb." While I heard those words, I never thought *too* much about it until I became an adult. Now, as a parent of eight children, I understand what *unique* actually means.

After being married and working for five years, my husband and I started our family with our first child, Anna. I had been a high school language arts teacher, and Matt had been working in the IT department for a food corporation for five years before getting approved to work remotely in Ohio, where our families were located. While Ohio was not a warm state, it was at least warmer than Minnesota, and our children would have the opportunity to know their relatives if we moved back.

God would continue to bless our family with nine more souls after Anna. Before Sarah, we had never had any trouble conceiving and were blessed with healthy children every time. Then, when we got pregnant in 2015, I noticed something was not right after about five weeks. We lost our sixth baby to a miscarriage. This was a *unique* experience for us, but we had friends who had suffered miscarriages and were able to reach out to them for consolation.

After a couple of months, we were ready to try again and got pregnant right away. Unfortunately, we also lost our seventh baby to miscarriage. After this experience, I sought some advice as to what may have caused the loss of these two precious children. Once I started on some vitamins and tried to get my body a little healthier, we were ready to try again. Sophia, our sixth living child, was our "rainbow" baby, born just 14 months after the loss of our first miscarried baby.

After Sophia was born in 2016, God blessed us with two more *unique* souls: Emma and William. In the throwaway society in which we live, it is *unique* to have eight children. Our oldest is nearly 14, and our youngest is six months. When we started our family, we thought maybe we would have five or six children at the most, but we cannot imagine our family life any other way.

One thing is certain: every family is *unique*. No two families are the same because no two people are the same. We have four daughters and four sons. Each one is special and also *unique*. We have brown eyes and blue eyes, brown hair and blonde hair, short children and tall children, loud children and quiet children, athletic children and artistic children, funny children and serious children—and plenty of healthy fighting to keep us always praying and asking God to help us understand the best way to raise them!

PART 6

The Never-ending Fruitful Garden

We have a 100-year-old rhododendron in our front yard. She majestically stands guard over our 100-year-older home. She's the queen of the neighborhood. And, though she is weathered, she is breathtakingly beautiful, especially when in full bloom in her purple robe.

Not only is she gorgeous; she's fun and strong! She's the very best climbing tree around. She has endured my seven sons and all their friends for 25 years and generations of children before that. She is stronger for giving her all! She has endured, extending her limbs to all, carrying and sheltering and raising high to the sky all those whom she embraces.

This matriarch of the garden is much like the women you will meet in this chapter, the "never-ending fertile gardens." Motherhood is much like being a fertile garden, only mothers harvest beautiful humans, not just flowers. The world needs more flowers…and more babies!

As we all journey the "mother" journey, let's remember the 100-year-older rhodie, continuing to hold the babies in our branches, deciding to live with open arms and hearts, sheltering all who want shade from the sun, raising all as high as they can climb, and always blooming…giving it our all, until our last breath.

Enjoy the remarkable women that you will meet in this chapter. You will read about women like 93-year-old Irene Grimm, who has mothered 17 children, and 141 grandchildren and over a hundred great grandchildren (and counting), and Angelica O'Reilly, mom of nine, who has started a line of wine with her four daughters.

Enjoy these strong matriarchs who not only mother and grandmother beautifully, but are solitaire cultural icons, showing us the way.

And may the seeds we plant, like the never-ending fruitful garden, bloom from generation unto generation.

Bloom on…

The Mother Garden

The more I've Mama'd
the more I love the garden.
The dark, musty, worm-infested soil,
That nourishes
And sustains life…
The humble earth
that welcomes the discarded,
that gleans the good
from the thrown away,
the broken, the abandoned,
and absorbs and transforms it all
into pure nourishment…

The garden is the fertile womb
that welcomes the tiny seeds,
holding and nourishing
the littlest ones
as they unfurl and bloom…

My lofty ambition,
at the end of the day,
is to be more like the simple garden,
as open and as welcoming
as God's fertile earth,
where the birds sing
and the flowers bloom
and there's always room
to breathe…
and always room
for more flowers.

If only I could live each day
where All are welcome
in my mother-garden.

A mother's arms are full of tenderness
and children sleep soundly in them.

– VICTOR HUGO

48

Maureen McPartland

Maureen is a teacher, nutritionist, and the mother of seven.

We were blessed with seven children in 10 years. Yes, they were close, and to this day, they remain very close. Chaos reigned much of the time, but it was a good chaos. Busyness, trials, tears, celebrations, laughter, and joy amongst dysfunction. Totally normal!

The kids learned to work hard on the farm, providing most of our labor force. Up early at 5:30 a.m. to change the water (siphon tubes, hundreds of them) be-

fore school. During the summer, they were again up early to beat the heat of the day, and spent time weeding beans, or alfalfa seed, and just doing what needed to be done. Piling into the pickup, some in the cab and some in the back, they'd head to the fields.

Another fast forward in our journey: our family has grown over the years from our seven children. God continues his blessings in our three beautiful, faith-filled daughters-

in-law and three very caring sons-in-law, and now, 20 grandchildren. Faith and family are foremost in the way they, too, raise their families. My husband gave his directive that when they all grew up, they could live anywhere in the world they wanted, as long as it was within an 80-mile radius of us. (They actually stretched it a bit; one family is about 150 miles away). Traveling the world is great, but: come home!

As we've reached our retirement years, God has given us another challenge. My fun-loving farmer husband, my children's beloved dad, has been diagnosed with Parkinson's disease. It's a nasty disease that has stripped away so much of his independence. We've had to retire from the farm, and we moved to Spokane to be near our four daughters and their families. Our sons and their families lend support with frequent phone calls or visits. My farmer isn't always a happy guy with the move to the city (you can take the man out of the country, but you can't take the country out of the man), but one thing that does cheer him (and at times overwhelms him) is his *family*.

It cheers him to see that his hard work on the farm paid off. It cheers him to see their interactions as friends, and as parents to our little grandchildren. And it thrills me to see the cousins together, wondering when they can get together next. The love of family, and the love of the farm life, continue. We, with God's help, grew a pretty good crop of independent, confident, caring individuals who share our own love of family, learning to work together and who, to this day, remain very close.

As for my part? I stand behind *all* 34 "spring offs" as one of their biggest fans and cheerleaders! I'm so extremely thankful for God's gift of family.

49

Nerissa Jimenez

Nerissa is a mother of three, a grandmother, business owner, and ministry leader.

Mothering is an art that we are always working on enhancing. Yes, we fall short, but we grow and evolve, many times right in front of our children, so they see our evolution. There are times in our journey as mothers that we want to "lose it." My mom used to say, "I am going to run down the street naked!" and I could not quite understand that until I had my own crew and I have felt that same feeling a time or two. I have also experienced an overwhelming feeling of gratitude that God would give me these beautiful people to love and parent. That feeling often brings tears to my eyes.

I have grown to learn that God has made them unique and special for His glory. I was speaking to a friend about our children, and she likened them to a bam-

boo shoot in the ground. All the roots are not seen but they are growing and developing under the dirt. The nutrients we give them, and their growth, cannot always be seen until a certain time when they break forth. Well, when they break through all that dirt, how beautiful they are and how amazing their growth is to behold. Some we will see sooner than others, but nonetheless, we will behold their beauty in the appointed seasons of life.

As a "stair-step" child, number three of six, my mother had us one to two years apart, and I had an interesting childhood. I would not trade it for anything and love being a part of a large family. We did everything together. When asked why she thought we are still so close, my mother said that she always encouraged us to embrace each other and others, especially when greeting. This was not a norm for my father, but something she insisted upon in our family.

As children of immigrants, we had certain standards and were aware of sacrifices that were made for us to live in the suburbs of New York. We experienced lack (coming from the area of Bedford Stuyvesant in Brooklyn, New York), as well as abundance—and I know that is what makes us more well-rounded today. We have a closeness that friends comment on often and tell us that our bond is different—a closeness that is beyond words. I know that I can count on my siblings, no matter the situation or circumstance, to be there for me. I have learned how unique our relationship is and I am thankful for it.

We bonded through adversity. Separation, sickness, and death eventually just brought us closer together. Our father experienced a car accident that required a full body cast and he slept in our living room in a hospital bed for a year during my teenager years. He struggled with diabetes, high blood pressure, and blindness at one point. Never in a million years did

my mother foresee having to care for her husband in these situations, but she did it while still seeing to us (most of the time).

We all took turns caring for him in one way or another. Some of us sacrificed so much, but it was instilled in us that we would care for each other. We tragically lost him at the young age of 52. We also lost our childhood family home, experienced diseases in our families such as leukemia, brain aneurysms, back and other surgeries, and yet God's hand has kept us alive, close as a family—and today we stand in triumph.

It is sometimes scary how much my life parallels my mother's, having to care for my spouse through illness and adversity—and experiencing the same awareness that love covers all and endures all. Understanding that even through times of great pain, or the realization that things will not happen the way envisioned, by the grace of God, we still held onto each other. My children continue to let me mother them with a loosened grip, and they would not have it any other way. Our job as a mother is never truly done. What I find most beautiful is seeing that love demonstrated generationally, through our children. They are close, take care of each other and, for a mother, it is a beautiful thing to watch.

50

Arlyn Lawrence

*Arlyn is an editor, writer, and the founder of Inspira Literary Solutions.
She has authored and co-authored several books, including* Prayer-Saturated Kids:
Equipping and Empowering Children in Prayer, *and*
Parenting for the Launch: Raising Teens to Succeed in the Real World.
Arlyn is the mother of five and grandmother of 11.

I don't remember which of my five pregnancies I announced to my husband with a mention of Psalm 128, but it was probably number four or five, which was when we realized we were starting to surpass the national average. "Your wife will be like a fruitful vine within your house; your children will be like olive shoots around your table." (Psalm 128:3)

I thought about that verse when I first heard the title for this book, *The Crowded Table*. Now, our grown and still-growing family numbers 22 when we are all together: as of this writing, four of the five are

married, with 11 children between them all, including two sets of twins. When we all get together, the table is indeed crowded!

There are so many benefits to a large family: the camaraderie. The community. The support. The delight. The joy. The satisfaction of knowing that one way you are changing the world is to help fill it with truly wonderful human beings who will make it a better place. And then to watch them do it—to find and fulfill their gifts and callings—that is the best!

Granted, there are certainly challenges involved in raising a large family. The drain on your physical and emotional energy. The frequent lack of personal space or time to yourself. The amount of money and time it takes to support and sustain a family comfortably in this day and age. The mental and emotional investment it takes to be involved in their lives, especially as they mature, become adults, and move out from under your roof and into the world (that's likely where a lot of our gray hairs come from!).

One way my husband Doug and I attempted to meet some of these challenges was to seek to understand God's design for each of our children as individuals, rather than just coming up with our own plans for them, or resorting to a "one-size-fits-all" form of parenting. We recognized that each child was a gift from God to us and to the world. Our job as parents has been, to the best of our abilities, to unwrap those gifts, learn their design and purpose, and release them into the world to accomplish God's purposes for them.

Therein lies one of the biggest challenges of parenting: if you have more than one child, you know that no two are alike—not even twins! (We have found this from personal experience as we have been blessed with TWO sets of twin grandbabies!) Children are a lot like snowflakes that way. One size does not necessarily fit all.

Among my own five, there is a broad spectrum of traits and characteristics. Number one is practical, dependable, and level-headed. My number two, almost in direct contrast, is free-spirited, idealistic, and independent. Number three is also very practical—capable and resilient. Number four, my most introverted and introspective, is also the deepest thinker and very insightful. Number five is a pronounced people-lover and loyal friend.

By temperament, I'm probably most like my number two. My husband is on the more laid back and methodical end of the spectrum. All seven of us complement each other in a number of ways. But, can you begin to imagine some of the sparks we've had over the years, because of our different combinations of personalities?

That's why understanding our children's (and our own) unique wiring is so important. Even the most well-intentioned parenting efforts in the world will fall short unless we have a strong relationship with our children that will allow our messages to get through. "Train up a child in the way he should go," says Proverbs 22:6, "and when he is old he will not depart from it." Raise him or her, that is, according to the child's natural bent.

Kids vary remarkably in their needs, reactions, communications, and behavioral styles, as do parents. Every child is unique and every parent is unique, and every parent-child relationship is distinctive, as well. Understanding this and using it to your advantage and not your detriment is especially key.

And *pray*. Ask God to show you His heart and plans for your children. No one knows our children (and grandchildren) like the One who made them, and He loves to give us His wisdom when we ask for it!

*"If any of you lacks wisdom, you should ask God,
who gives generously to all without finding fault, and
it will be given to you."*

JAMES 1:5

51

Angelica O'Reilly

🌿

Angela is a mother of eight, a winery founder,
and the owner of Owen Roe Winery in Washington State.

Motherhood is one of the greatest privileges and joys in life. There is no substitute for the love and friendship between you and your children.

My wonderful husband, David, and I brought eight lives into this world to love always and unconditionally. Wanting a certain style of life and inclined to living and working off the land, we settled on entering the wine business, and it has been an incredible, ongoing journey. A family business allows for individual and communal growth—physical, emotional, and spiritual. It's not the easiest thing to calmly resolve issues that arise daily with the people you know most intimately. Real maturity grows from navigating these issues and, at the end of the day, reconciling with anyone that may have been offended.

David and I founded Owen Roe Winery in Washington State in 1999. From the very beginning, everything we did included babies in carriers or toddlers at our sides. Soon they were part of the day-to-day chores, walking the vineyards to making wine. In the high school years, we insisted they work for us, not to force them into the wine industry, but to instill responsibility and a work ethic they could bring to any future career. They did harvesting, processing grapes, winemaking, and bottling as well as sales. During their college years, the

kids would bring in friends to work summers or early harvests.

Dominic, our eldest, was already equal to the task of winemaking even before college. After college, Dominic travelled to New Zealand, California, and Australia to acquire additional and diverse experience in winemaking, eventually settling in California with his wife, Anna. Together with their family of soon-to-be-six children, they continue the adventures of a winemaking family, adding cidery to the mix.

, Eamonn, now in his first year of college, worked in the vineyards and cellar through high school. When home, he helps with labeling, bottling, and shipping . He was also a tremendous help in getting our building ready. The youngest two boys, Cormie and Dodie, have helped in bottling and shipping, but mostly just love our coffee breaks.

Our daughters, Brigid, Moira, and Me-Z were at the right place in life when we needed to plant new vineyards on a rocky hillside. Countless hours were spent digging and wrapping "grow tubes" on acres of vines. And there were also quiet hours spent in the tasting room, sharing the fruits of their labor with customers.

After graduating from college, Brigid and Moira each went their own ways. Then the pandemic hit. Brigid, Moira, and Me-Z, studying in Rome, all returned to the U.S. Together with Rosie, just finishing high school, we all decided to launch a new business: Distaff Wine Company.

"Distaff" refers to the female's side of the family and her ancestry. The name seemed appropriate. Each of us, mother and daughters, with our unique gifts, decided to put our talents together to form a new wine company. Mom, with 30 years of experience, concentrates on the "big picture," and overall direction. Brigid directs sales and media promotions. Moira manages hospitality, events, and shipping. Me-Z, the gifted artist, does the artwork for our labels, advertising, and murals. She is also our lead photographer and videographer. Rosie graduated from being the "Coffee Girl" to being a real part of our team in promotions and shipping.

It's an exciting and fun adventure to start a winery with your adult daughters. I'm so proud of the women they have become: intelligent, independent, caring, joyful, and fun-loving. They are vintners, writers, photographers, videographers, storytellers, and the most gracious hosts.

Our time spent together is a channel for us to grow together. The challenges are real, but because we all are working towards the same end—personal growth, and holiness—we try to be better people every day. This means while getting the job done, we allow for each other's shortcomings as well as strengths. As a mom, I am also grateful for the continual opportunities for my own growth.

God gave us each other, to journey together toward our final end. With our youngest now 13, I see this very clearly. I am eternally grateful for the challenges, hardships, sufferings, joys, accomplishments…everything, because I fear what we would have been without them!

52

Irene Grimm

Irene is the mother of 17, grandmother to 141, and a cultural icon of mothering many.

It would give me great pleasure to be able to write that I had made a decision to have many children. Truth to tell, it was more of an expectation, an openness to the possibility of a big family. As a 17-year-old bride in 1947, my concept of a large family was formed by my parents' family of nine, and my two married sisters, who had six and four children respectively. I recall shocking a group of friends in high school

by stating that I hoped to have seven children. Even back then, at my Catholic girls' school, seven children seemed outrageous to them—certainly not something one would *choose*. I'm not sure where I got that number: maybe I couldn't imagine competing with Mom, but I hoped to at least one-up my sisters!

Apparently, I am very competitive. Two of my five sisters had mega-families, 14 and 16, so I kept up and then surpassed them to 17 children! Seriously, though, there was no sense of competition, but gratitude as the openness to God's plan brought us one beautiful, healthy baby after another. My children all grew to be mature, caring, responsible adults, men and women destined for God's glory. Two of them are already before the Lord's mercy.

There were certainly challenges along the way, but now that I am 91, and cared

for by these lovely people God was so good as to send me, I can only be grateful for His abundant Providence. I have 17 children and 16 wonderful children-in-law, 141 grandchildren, and 157 great grand-children (and at least six more on the way!), each of them beautiful and precious to me. I've been especially gratified by the fact that my children and now my grandchildren are open to big families—my husband and I must have done something right! I could not have dreamed such abundance for myself back when I began married life. I am so grateful that, by the example of my good parents and sisters, I was open to the incredible gifts God had in store for me.

PART 7

Science Speaks:

MOTHERING MANY MAKES YOU HAPPIER, HEALTHIER, AND LONGER-LIVED

Want to be happier? Healthier? Live longer? Then have many children! The latest scientific discoveries tell us that science is finally catching up.

Global scientific studies concur that women who mother many are happier, healthier, and live longer. This is amazing! This needs to be shouted from the rooftops. Culture has tried to tell women that they will be mentally, emotionally, and physically destroyed by having lots of children when, in reality, the reverse is true! My own great-grandmother, Eva Thaden, mother of 10, was a tiny but fiery, spirited force until she passed away at 98.

Dr. Bronwyn Harman, at the Edith Cowan University, in Australia, finds that parents with four or more children are the happiest parents.[1] Dr. Harman spent five years studying different kinds of families and collecting data. She says, "We think it's because they purposefully planned to have a large family, and while they report stressors such as chaos, noise, and financial difficulties, this is outweighed by the joy the family brings to the household."

---

[1] Ellen Sturm Niz September 14, 2015. (n.d.). "Happiest Parents Have Four or More Kids, Study Says." *Parents*. Retrieved February 6, 2022, from https://www.parents.com/toddlers-preschoolers/everything-kids/happiest-parents-have-four-or-more-kids-study-says/

Scientists have also recently found women who mother many are healthier, emotionally and physically, and live longer. According to the National Cancer Institute (NCI), women who have children are less likely to develop breast and uterine cancer. Being pregnant reduces exposure to certain hormones that have been linked to breast cancer (due to the fact that menstruation stops when a woman is pregnant). The NCI also reports that breastfeeding can reduce breast cancer risk because the "maturing that breast cells go through in order to produce milk may prevent cells from becoming cancerous."[2]

Recent science has discovered the amazing health benefits that babies' fetal cells provide the mother. The fetal cells can migrate to damaged tissue and repair it in the mother.[3] (Fetal cells have been proven to help heal Caesarean section wounds.)

Yep, this means that many mothers have some cells from their kids embedded throughout their bodies.

A 2014 Danish study published in the *International Journal of Epidemiology* suggests that male microchimerism is associated with a lower mortality rate in women. During pregnancy, a woman and her fetus exchange small quantities of cells, and their persistence later is termed microchimerism.

A study out of Canada's Simon Fraser University suggests that having more kids slows moms' aging process. Research shows that the more children a woman has, the longer her telomeres (the protective ends of our DNA) are. Telomere shortening is linked to our aging. The longer our telomeres are, the slower we age! Having more children keeps us young!![4]

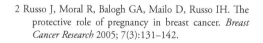

2 Russo J, Moral R, Balogh GA, Mailo D, Russo IH. The protective role of pregnancy in breast cancer. *Breast Cancer Research* 2005; 7(3):131–142.

3 *Vital Statistics Rapid release.* (n.d.). Retrieved February 6, 2022, from https://www.cdc.gov/nchs/data/vsrr/vsrr012-508.pdf

4 Barha, C. K., Hanna, C. W., Salvante, K. G., Wilson, S. L., Robinson, W. P., Altman, R. M., & Nepomnaschy, P. A. (2016). Number of children and telomere length in women: A prospective, longitudinal evaluation. PLOS ONE, 11(1). https://doi.org/10.1371/journal.pone.0146424

Researchers in Israel found that both mice and humans exhibited faster tissue rejuvenation after pregnancy. The fetal cells that mingle with the mother's organs and bloodstream may act like an "injection of youth."[5] And, a 2012 Australian study, as well as studies in Israel and Norway, have shown that the risk of death was lower for women who had four or more children during the studies.

Finally, while science has shown that women who mother many are happier, healthier, and live longer, science also proves that having more children is beneficial for mothers' mental health in later life. In *Aging and Mental Health*, published in June 2020, researcher Thijs van den Broek suggests that because of the support, caretaking, and connection that women with big families have as they age, they have less depression and slower mental health declines.

Having many children just may be the fountain of youth!

5   Falick Michaeli, T., Laufer, N., Sagiv, J. Y., Dreazen, A., Granot, Z., Pikarsky, E., Bergman, Y., & Gielchinsky, Y. (2015, August). *The rejuvenating effect of pregnancy on muscle regeneration.* Aging cell. Retrieved February 6, 2022, from https://www.ncbi.nlm.nih.gov/pmc/articles/PMC4531083/

Afterword

"I believe the world will be saved by beauty."
- Fyodor Dostoyevsky

The Crowded Table is one hundred percent a celebration of the dignity of women, of every woman! This book erases the line between women who work outside the home and those who work inside the home. Let's face it: we *all* work, all the time. Motherhood erases all lines and borders; it is the unconditional love and commitment to relationships that our divisive world is so hungry for!

This book is just a small part of the ongoing conversation. So much more global dialogue, collaboration, and civilized discourse are needed. Dialogue, in a spirit of love, can help change the world!

As we conclude this glimpse into the bravery and the beauty of daring to mother many in this age of fewer babies, I hope you have had a glimpse of, and perhaps felt a stirring toward, what every woman in these pages has said in one way or another:

- that by giving your life away, you get it back, a hundredfold
- that there is a life that is greater and sweeter and wilder than the world can ever define or measure
- that there is something Beyond, something more sacrificial but more satisfying than awards and applause and financial compensation, something that brings greater happiness than any THING there is.

It is Love.
It is relationships.
It is the sweet spot of life
and it's only found by giving one's heart away,
by laying down one's life,
by sacrificing and serving.

Children and family are a glorious, challenging, delightful path to this Beauty and Happiness…the Beyond. Beauty, joy, fullness, and ABUNDANCE await!!!

Authentic beauty…unlocks the yearning of the human heart,
the profound desire to know, to love,
to go toward the Other, to reach for the Beyond.

— *BENEDICT XVI*

About the Author

Angela Connelly is a passionate, multi-tasking mom of nine who finds joy in the chaos of mothering many. She is a graduate of Thomas Aquinas College, where she is now a member of the Board of Governors. She is the founder and former president of Washington Women's Network, a legislative lobbying group focused on women and children, and serves on the board of various local and national nonprofits focusing on women, children, and fighting homelessness. Angela is a previous community coordinator for the University of Washington, as well as a young adults pastoral minister to 19 Catholic Churches of Pierce County deanery.

Currently, Angela's most active passion project is a community-focused organization she founded: Tacoma Safe. It works to keep her beloved community of Tacoma safe, healthy, and thriving by providing resources related to crime prevention, homelessness, and more.

Angela loves her family, faith, children, and growing flowers. She and her husband, Jack, live in the Pacific Northwest, raising their nine rowdy children and enjoying their four granddaughters (with one more granddaughter on the way)! She laughs daily at the crazy joy she gets to experience because of the blessing of abundance and saying "yes" to Jesus.

Throughout her life, Angela has been enamored and inspired by the concept of a crowded table. She has always wanted to open her home, her table, and her heart to those who need a mother's love—related by blood or otherwise. No matter the storm, she finds deep joy in mothering many and serving her crowded a table at which all are welcome.

www.angelaconnelly.com

CPSIA information can be obtained
at www.ICGtesting.com
Printed in the USA
JSHW011549250522
26344JS00001B/3